MITCHELL-LUKER'S ARRAN BUS BOOK

This book is dedicated to my good friend

GEORGE MUNRO, omnibus driver retired

MITCHELL-LUKER'S ARRAN BUS BOOK

The history of the omnibus and coaching services in the Island of Arran 1830–1980

KILBRANNAN PUBLISHING LIMITED

First published 1983 by Kilbrannan Publishing Ltd., Brodick, Isle of Arran, Scotland.

ISBN 0 907939 06 6

Mitchell-Luker, B
  Mitchell-Lukers' Arran bus book.
  1. Coaching——Scotland——Arran——History
  2. Motor bus lines——Scotland—Arran—History
  I. Title
  388.3'22'0941461   HE5665.A/

  ISBN 0-907939-06-6

Designed, illustrated and phototypeset by Kilbrannan Publishing Limited, Brodick, Isle of Arran, Scotland.
Printed in Great Britain by The Moxon Press Limited.

The writer has no connection with the transport or tourism industry.

CONTENTS

	Page
INTRODUCTION TO MAINLAND OMNIBUSES	11
THE ISLE OF ARRAN	15
McBRIDE, Brodick	21
HIRERS & DRIVERS	24
CURRIE, Shiskine	44
BLACKWATERFOOT—BRODICK COMPETITORS	54
RIBBECK, Brodick	57
KERR-NEWTON, Brodick	65
HAMILTON, High Kildonan	69
JAMIESON, Low Kildonan	72
McNEILL, Kildonan	75
ROLLS-ROYCE — A Five Year Search	78
CURRIE, Kilmory	81
STEWART, Corriecravie, Whiting Bay	83
SHISKINE, LAGG & SOUTH COAST RAILWAY	89
LENNOX, Whiting Bay, Lamlash & Brodick	95
ANDERSON, Whiting Bay	106
BOLT, Lamlash	108
GORDON BROS, Lamlash, Kildonan	110
CANNON, Lamlash	119
THE KING'S CROSS OMNIBUSES	123
McMILLAN, Pirnmill	130
ANDERSON, Pirnmill	132
CLARK, Lochranza	135
ROBERTSON, Blackwaterfoot	137
McMILLAN, Blackwaterfoot	140

Page

WEIR, Machrie.. 142
BANNATYNE MOTORS, Blackwaterfoot................. 147
UP TO DATE 151
"ARRAN COACHES"—All Arran 153
POSTBUS, Brodick.................................... 164
BUS SHELTERS...................................... 175
AND FINALLY — 177
APPENDIX 1: Tickets 181
APPENDIX 2: Timetables............................. 184
APPENDIX 3: Concessionary Travel.................... 191
ACKNOWLEDGEMENTS 195

LIST OF PLATES

(1) The Brodick—Corrie road, 1904.
(2) Glen Rosa, 1906.
(3) Pre-motor road in the King's Cross district.
(4) The String Road, c.1949.
(5) Post–1929 Bridge at Lamlash.
(6) Brodick Pier, 1908.
(7) Whiting Bay Pier, 1908.
(8) A Gordon's Albion at Whiting Bay, 1932.
(9) Brodick 1960s. Bannatyne Albion, Weir Commer, Ribbeck Albion, Ribbeck Commer TS3, Bannatyne Leyland Comet.
(10) ATT Fleet. Alistair Nicholson.
(11) Currie horse brake at Shiskine, 1905.
(12) Lennox hire carriage, c.1911.
(13) Hamilton's brake at Lagg, 1889.
(14) Willie Currie's mail cart off its usual route, above Lamlash, 1908.
(15) Jamieson, Kildonan, 1909.
(16) Stewart, Corriecravie, 1897.
(17) CMLR urban operation.
(18) What might have been CMLR rural operation.
(19) The first motor car in Arran.

(20) The first motor omnibus in Arran — Colin Currie's 1913 Albion.

(21) Bolt's 1918 GMC SJ222 at King's Cross c.1925 with George Moore and Maggie Smith behind McNeish's van.

(22) Stewart's first T–Ford on the Ross.

(23) Ribbeck's Albion 'Viking'.

(24) Colin Currie's road-breaking Albion, 1925.

(25) Made in Guildford, body fitted in Wishaw—Stewart's first Dennis, a 14–seater, SJ521.

(26) Lennox Chevrolet. On the back seat, in black, 'Greetin' Kate'.

(27) Charabancs — probably McRae Brothers at Shiskine, c.1928.

(28) A Ribbeck Albion 'The Valkyrie', with overflow starting tour.

(29) Hughie MacKenzie with McNeill Rolls-Royce at Whiting Bay, c.1928.

(30) Gunboat Smith and (pre-Arran) McNeill Rolls-Royce.

(31) Jimmy Anderson of Whiting Bay, charabanc c.1928.

(32) A Robertson Thorneycroft on the way to Arran, 1930.

(33) Two drivers with Stewart's 1937 Bedford WTB 25–seater.

(34) John Hamilton, David Middleton, Ian Martin and Sam Ross washing 14–seat Chevrolets in the burn, 1932.

(35) Lennox Bedford Saloon.

(36) Anderson's Berliet and McMillan's Ford at Pirnmill.

(37) 1931 Lennox Bedford.

(38) 1931 Lennox Bedford.

(39) Hammie Kerr with 'Silver Bullet'.

(40) 'Silver Bullet' with passengers.

(41) Weir's interchangeable Albion, 1934.

(42) The 'new' Morris mail vans outside the—then—Post Office, Brodick, 1936/37.

(43) Ticket rack and clipper, 'Setright' ticket machine.

(44) Ribbeck's 1937 Commer 'Avenger'.

(45) Hamilton Kerr with a visitor—A. Lennox (son of 'Pa').

(46) Donald Robertson.

(47) Bannatyne Motors Leyland Comet.

(48) Lennox's Leyland Comet.

(49) Bannatyne Motors Foden omnibus.

(50) Lennox's Foden omnibus.

(51) Ian MacKenzie with Lennox half-cab Leyland.

(52) Ribbeck's half-cab Albion at Lochranza, 1961.

(53) Lennox machines at Brodick, 607–AEC & 711–Foden.

(54) Weir's 1947 half-cab Albion, known locally as 'The Train', with two Bedfords on the left, at Machrie.

(55) Peter McMillan, Archie Currie, Colin Currie, Rab Hume, Nicol Currie, George Munro.
(56) Hughie MacKenzie and friends.
(57) McMillan Commer before sale to Lennox.
(58) McMillan Commer after sale to Lennox.
(59) Gordon's Albion, c.1938.
(60) Bannatyne Motors Foden.
(61) Douglas Kerr, the first motor-hirer in East Arran.
(62) Lennox utility Bedford.
(63) Weir's of Machrie Bedfords: 29–seat OB; 11–seat Dormobile.
(64) Ribbeck's Morris 12–seat Minibus.
(65) The Lennox depot, Whiting Bay, c.1929.
(66) The Lennox Garage, Lamlash.
(67) John Smith, Elizabeth Arnott and Duncan Weir.
(68) Interchange at Lochranza, 1966.
(69) A Lennox Albion, used for touring during the 1960s.
(70) Ribbeck Tour at Machrie, 1966.
(71) Scottish Aviation body Fodens at Blackwaterfoot.
(73) Ribbeck and Weir vehicles at Lochranza.
(74) Lennox OB Bedford at Lochranza, 1966.
(75) The ex-Devon General/Grey Cars Bannatyne Motors semi-automatic AEC Regal.
(76) Lennox SB Bedford.
(77) Supplementary route indicator.
(78) Dodge Postbus 716 at Brodick with driver John McBride.
(79) Land Rover Postbus at Blackwaterfoot.
(80) Postbus No.319 at Blackwaterfoot with driver Alice Lennox.
(81) Fergie Latona and Jack Lennox.
(82) Donny Campbell.
(83) Post Office drivers.
(84) Louis Joss in Commer Postbus No.493 at Shannochie, 1979.
(85) An ATT Bedford SB Bella Vega.
(86) George McKechnie.
(87) Danny Stewart in 139 at Whiting Bay, Winter 1981.
(88) 16–seat Ford Minibus, Willowbrook body.
(89) ATT No.400 — a dual purpose cuss or boach.
(90) ATT coach.
(91) The Old Grey Mare, ATT 783.
(92) ATT drivers.
(93) ATT 459 coming off the steamer.

(94) The hired coach OPT594M, 1978.
(95) Passing, near Machrie, 1982.
(96) Phil Broomhead in 351 at Blackwaterfoot.
(97) Negotiating Corrie road works.
(98) Driving in to Arran High School, Lamlash.
(99) The mass departure from Arran High School.
(100) Andy Lane's Lamlash 'depot' — the car park in the White House woods.
(101) Postbus No.717 climbing to Lavencorrach.
(102) Coming down again.
(103) Two visitors at the Community Arts shelter, 1982.
(104) The Wilkinson shelter.
(105) Rear view of 138.
(106) Rear view of 845.
(107) Danny Craig.
(108) Visitors to Arran for 40 years.
(109) Grant Weir & Bruce Hough.
(110) Danny Stewart.
(111) Alistair Nicholson.
(112) Alastair MacBride.
(113) Ernest Gordon.
(114) Bedford/Plaxton 45–seater driven by Alastair MacBride, 1981.
(115) Awaiting the morning rush, 1982.
(116) Lennox's Brodick 'depot', c.1954.
(117) The fact-finding committee.
(118) Ralston Green, 1982.
(119) Col. Currie, 1908 and Phil Broomhead, 1982.
(120) The new 'tram' and Kevin Kilshaw.

INTRODUCTION
TO MAINLAND OMNIBUSES

OMNIBUS: A Latin word, also used by the French, meaning: 'For everyone'.

OMNIBUS: A long 4-wheeled public transport vehicle, with seats along the sides and entrance at the rear. In some cases, the vehicle has additional seats on the roof. Omnibuses usually ply along stated routes, and the term, by statute, in Great Britain, is used to refer to vehicles carrying passengers at pre-arranged and individually-charged fares along a set route at advertised times.

The above definitions are taken from an American dictionary printed in 1929. I chose a foreign but English-speaking dictionary because I wanted to see how foreigners see us, and I chose 1929 because British omnibuses were 100 years old in that year. (To be more precise, they were 'officially' 100 years old that year).

The word 'omnibus' has been shortened to 'bus' through the years. Charles Dickens seems to be mainly responsible for that; I'll endeavour to correct the matter during the course of this book, and use the word 'bus' only where it is part of a company title, or where I am quoting verbatim the words of someone else. The word is, in any case, mis-applied to many vehicles, just as the word 'coach' is mis-applied to many omnibuses. An omnibus must carry its passengers as individuals, and although these individuals may all get on to the omnibus at the same time, and just one of them asks for, and pays for, 'Six and two halves to the High Street' the actual tickets are issued in the form of six and two, not in the form of, or in respect of, a lump sum. For this reason, although I have used the expression in this book for convenience the term 'school bus' is incorrect, since the passengers are carried by the operator for a lump sum which often accrues over a period of months and is not paid at the time.

The word 'coach' is often misused as well; the word itself is taken from the Hungarian town of Kocs, where the first comfortable passenger vehicle was built in the 15th century.

For the purpose of this book, any vehicle used on a regular, time-tabled run, on which individually-levied fares are charged, is an omnibus, be it a utility 'bus' or Danny Stewart's coach, and any vehicle used for a 'one off-trip to the Castle' by the Womens' Rural, or to take the Darts Club to another part of the island by special arrangement, is a coach, as is any vehicle used on a regular tour, and this holds good for Danny Stewart's luxurious, comfortable 'coach', and just as good if a service 'bus' is taken off its scheduled run at the last minute (a favourite but, fortunately, not too regular Arran Transport trick) to give a party of tourists a hurl round the island as arranged by just one of them direct with the company.

Omnibuses go back much further than this book will, but a brief history will not, I think, come amiss here.

Omnibuses were invented by a mathematician called Pascall, and placed in service on the streets of Paris by him in the early 1660s. At that time, there were a series of Letters Patent and Royal Decrees forbidding 'soldiers and peasants' to travel in them. No doubt the idea caught on in other places, but as far as Great Britain is concerned, it was to be 150 years before, as Charles Dickens has it " — the appearance of the first omnibus caused the public mind to go in a new direction and prevented a great many Hackney cabs from going in any direction at all."

There was, in London, a coachbuilder named George Shillibeer, who received orders, from time to time, to build carriages to a certain design for a French 'omnibus company'. He saw the possibilities for such vehicles in London and decided to divert an order from France and use it himself. Up to that time, there had been nothing like a regular short-distance stage carriage in Britain, except possibly in certain cases I'll suggest in due course. Town transport was either in the shape of privately-owned (and privately-used) carriages, or in the form .of what we would call a 'taxi' today. Shillibeer realised the advantages of a 'set time' and 'set route' principle and he may well have realised the advantage to all concerned of the 'set fare' principle as well, since it was not uncommon for arguments between passengers and cab-men to end in violence when discussing the fare to be paid for the journey which had been taken. Another advantage to him was that he would not have a vehicle running empty or standing idle, with only four fares at most per trip to any one of a hundred and more destinations. His passengers would go to him — and more than four at a time — so he placed an advertisement in a London newspaper and on 4th, July 1829, the British omnibus industry was officially born. The idea was copied quickly by other people in London and elsewhere, and poor old George was soon driven out of business by competitors, although the omnibuses of London were, for a time, known as 'Shillibeers'. This practice soon died out, however, when shortly after leaving the omnibus industry George Shillibeer became an undertaker and patented a new type of hearse, known as a "Shillibeer".

Since neither Burns nor McGonagle had anything to say about them, we must turn again to Dickens, who was not only there at the time but made a close study of London 'Busses'. He wrote of:

"......the gaudiness of its exterior, the perfect simplicity of its interior and the native coolness of its cad".

"We are of the opinion," he said, "that of all known vehicles, from the glass coach in which we are taken to be christened, to that sombre caravan in which we must one day make our last journey, there is nothing like an omnibus."

In *Sketches by Boz* Dickens describes the rapid deterioration in the standards and morals of London 'busmen; by 1835 their behaviour in general was such that the nickname 'cad' used to describe omnibus conductors had passed into everyday usage and was applied to anyone who indulged in loutish and uncouth behaviour.

The time eventually came when 'improvement peered beneath the fustian, and under the aprons' of the omnibuses, and the various regulations passed in the 1840s improved the standards of London omnibus crews to the extent that:

"......that eloquent and sage body, the magistrates of London, were deprived of half their amusement and half their occupation".

Local authorities licensed omnibus crews in London and elsewhere until the period 1930–1980, when the Traffic Commissioners licensed omnibus crews, and after which period no licence is required for a conductor.

The men who pioneered mainland omnibuses — Shillibeer, Tilling

& Co. are now forgotten by all save a few historians — Shillibeer himself has been lying in St. Mary's churchyard, Chigwell, for more than a century, and a mile from his last resting place a new development 'Shillibeer Walk' on the site where his house once stood, is supposed, locally, to be named after an otherwise forgotten Chigwell Urban District Council member. To those who want the complete but not too long History of British Bus Services I recommend the book of that title by John Hibbs. Meantime, in Arran, the history is slightly different; the omnibuses here did not fall into the hands of large combines with offices 50 miles and more away. The Arran omnibus pioneers did it their way, as we shall see.

Lamlash, Summer 1938. Omnibus stopping to set down standing passengers. Greetin' Kate: "Of course I can get on, there are lots of seats in the coach." Conductress: "Aye, pet, lots, and every one with a bottom on it."

THE ISLE OF ARRAN

Most of the books of this type I have read either go into great detail about the history and location of the area with which they deal, or pre-suppose that the reader has a knowledge of the area. I do not propose to do either. Instead I have appended to this book a list of publications which will keep those of you who wish to make an in-depth study of Arran and its history busy for several years.

Meantime, and for those who do not have the inclination to make the said in-depth study —

The Isle of Arran is the largest island in the Firth of Clyde, on the west coast of Scotland. It is 165 square miles in area, with a population varying, between 1860 and 1980, of around 4,000. It is four miles to the east of the Kintyre peninsula of Argyllshire and 16 miles to the west of the Ayrshire coast. Until recently it was served by steamers from the Ayrshire coast which called at Whiting Bay (pier), King's Cross (rowing boat connection), Lamlash (pier), Brodick (pier) and Corrie (rowing boat connection) and in addition had rowing boat connections from Machrie and Pirnmill, and a pier at Lochranza giving inter-change facilities with steamers which plied between Campbeltown, Carradale and Glasgow. These are all gone now and the current position is that a steamer calls regularly several times each day at Brodick, from where it runs to Ardrossan on the Ayrshire coast. From Ardrossan to Carlisle by road is 98 miles. A milepost by the side of the railway line at Ardrossan, the start of a rather Chestertonian route by rail to Glasgow, gives the distance as 32 miles from Ardrossan South Beach to Glasgow Central Station.

There is also a summer service of steamers from Lochranza to the Kintyre coast, provided by a rather 'landing craft' looking vessel, from which I expect to see John Wayne leading the Marines ashore at any time. This connects with a Postbus service to Tarbert, Argyllshire.

Arran was, until recently, in the County of Bute; it is now in the Cunninghame District of the Strathclyde Region.

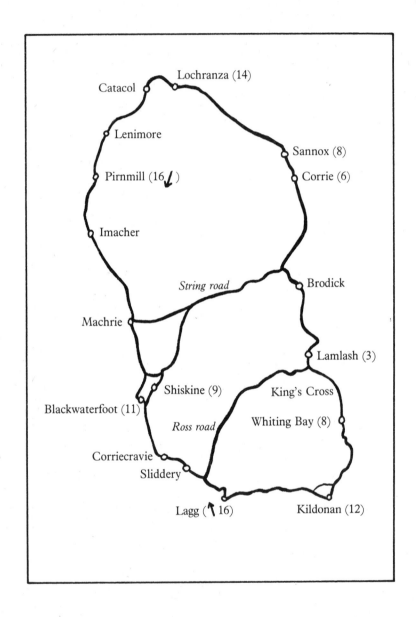

The numbers shown in brackets with the place names on the map opposite indicate mileages from Brodick, with arrows where necessary showing the shortest route. There is a series of sandstone knee-high columns alongside the road at intervals of a mile, clockwise round the island, showing the distance in miles from a point (M) at the Brodick Castle wall where King Edward landed in 1902. All mileages shown here, however, are taken from the distances indicated on the MOT signs by Brodick Pier, and from omnibus trip meters either given to me by various omnibus drivers (thanks lads!) or taken from the meters by me.

(There was one time when I was of unwitting service to Louis Joss, the south Arran postbus driver. In fact he told me "having you breathing down my neck is all I needed"!!)

Seriously, though, the distances shown here are approximate; for instance, I have recorded the information on the first road sign out of Brodick as 'Lamlash 3' but to what part of Lamlash that refers I cannot say.

This book goes back to the time when the traveller in Arran had to make his own way, because the way was not yet made.

Although the date 1830 in the title suggests a point at which the story begins, it is necessary to go back a bit further to look briefly at the birth of the modern road system which had taken place about 20 years previously. An account of the way in which roads were built and maintained at that time can be found in several of the books I mention elsewhere; from the Waywarden's point of view in *Lorna Doone,* from the point of view of the men who provided the labour in *Telford* and from the point of view of the historian (who, in the case I'm thinking of, is rather biased against the landowner — but otherwise accurate) in Robert McLellan's complete and all-embracing *The Isle of Arran* (David & Charles). In brief, and throughout Britain, at around that time, tenants of local landowners were required by law to spend a few days in each year making or maintaining roads. The number of days varied from place to place, owing to the requirement of Factors and Bailiffs as local circumstances dictated, which sometimes led to the imposition of several extra days' labour in place of a fine which might otherwise have been imposed in respect of some breach — real or imagined — of a tenant's missive of let. The 'Statute Labour' was abolished gradually in Britain but at the time of which I am writing it was in force.

At the end of the 18th century Arran's roads were little more than tracks, with gates across them where the road crossed the boundary of a farm or holding. With a spasmodic and unreliable, but for the period acceptable, form of transport in the shape of sailing boats to and from the mainland, and inter-village trading depending only upon pack-horses, there was no need for anything better until the end of the first decade of the 19th century, by which time several wheeled carts had been introduced to the island. The number of such vehicles in Arran increased to the point where Statute Labour, even with extra days as referred to, became unworkable on its own, so in 1810 the practice of using government and landowners' money to pay for 'professional labour' spread to Arran, and on the map on p.19 the section of road shown in thick black line, between Lamlash and Brodick, was built with the foreseeable increase in wheeled traffic in mind. Brodick as we know it today has its centre two miles to the south of the site of the old village served by this road in the early 19th century.

The way over the island from Brodick to Blackwaterfoot, shown here by means of a dot and long dash, was surveyed and planned by Thomas Telford, and built in 1817 by a contractor who subsequently made an annual charge to the landowner in respect of maintenance. In the same year, the road from Brodick to Sannox was laid to the point at which the dots indicating it cease and the Rev. Dr. D. Landsborough was to record 25 years later that it was not possible to take a wheeled carriage beyond Sannox in the direction of Loch Ranza. In 1822 a road was built from Lamlash to a point on the other side of the island (long dashes). There were other isolated and completely detached sections of road in the island, shown here by two thin lines, which were in existence by 1845. These were joined together by sections shown here as single thin lines by 1851. The section between Sannox and Lochranza was completed in 1843 but, as we shall see shortly, it was unequal to the task of supporting a four-ton charabanc 80 years later. Bridges, where there were any, were flimsy wooden structures built alongside shallow places in the burns, and horse-drawn vehicles forded the burns at those points while passengers crossed by the bridge. Stone-built bridges to bear the roads, many of which are still in

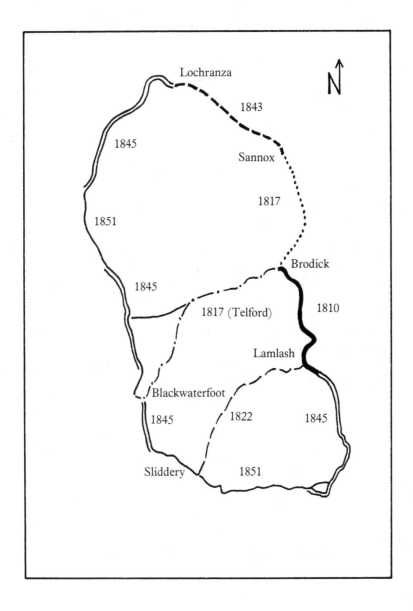

use, were constructed to a programme initiated in 1929.

After 1930 the then Ministry of Transport devised a system of numbering of one or more roads into routes. The system, which gets more logical the nearer one gets to London, gave the coastal roads of Arran the number A841, and the String Road the number B880. The Ross, Machrie Moor and Kildonan Low Roads do not appear to have any numbers at all, although I am sure that the Strathclyde Regional Council Roads Department will follow through the practice of the last few years and erect some signs in time.

The sketch maps used in this book are based on the road system as it was in 1976, at least, as Arran Transport (from whose timetable I traced it) saw the road system in 1976. The maps are 'near enough' for our purpose, since this book will not concern itself with any road not used by omnibuses. One or two changes have taken place in the years since the 'modern' road system appeared in 1850. There have been widening schemes, re-alignments, bends have been cut off — it is possible to see stretches of the early metalled road alongside the 'new bits' which have been re-located to the side of the old route taken. The number of side roads, mostly un-metalled and serving one or two farms, is such that, if put end to end from the junction with the main road shown on the map to the farm served, they would nearly double the length of all metalled roads joined together.

A London bus driver booked a holiday for a fortnight in Arran but went right past the hotel without stopping.

McBRIDE, Brodick

Brodick — Lamlash
Brodick — where required

Before suggesting that Mr. McBride was 15 years in advance of George Shillibeer, let me make it clear that I spent my formative years in the shadow of Shillibeer's house in Chigwell, (a) before they pulled it down, and (b) after mid-day, since our house was to the east of his. I sat under the memorial tablet erected by London busmen to Shillibeer's memory (and, of course, to the Glory of God) on the inside wall of St. Mary's Church, Chigwell — to which Charles Dickens made Barnaby Rudge run to ring the bell —through Matins and Evensong for many years. I weeded Shillibeer's grave in the churchyard for many years after the Sexton had ceased to do so, and for many years before the London Transport Board decided to make a ceremony of it. For want of knowledge of other ways to the hearts of a series of young women in the parish, I took them to see both tablet and grave of the great man, and wrote a letter of complaint to the *Daily Telegraph,* the General Post Office and the *Chigwell Times* when the 1979 Shillibeer 150th year was not commemorated by a special stamp in honour of his 'invention'.

When, owing to a system of estate management accepted as natural at the time and best forgotten except for the lessons to be learned today, Mr. McBride (his forename has not survived) found himself minus the farm on which he had earned his living, but still with a household to support, he imported a cart with spring suspension and seats from the mainland and 'hired it out'.

Mr. McBride lived in Brodick, which in 1814 was a small hamlet, with the slightly larger group of houses known as Invercloy between the original Brodick and the centre of what we now know by that name. Although vessels put into a small quay at the foot of the Castle wall, there was a harbour — formed by nature, not man — to the south at Lamlash. To this had been added in 1750, at a cost of £3,000, a stone jetty. As many as 300 ships in any one day could be seen in the natural harbour protected by Holy Island, which keeps the worst of the weather out of Lamlash Bay. The quay was demolished in a very short time after it had been built to provide material for building in the village, and it was 1872 before a replacement in the shape of a pier at Brodick was built. (The pier at Lamlash was built in 1883).

Even so, a series of ferry services was operated by sailing craft from Saltcoats, most of which called regularly at Lamlash. No record can be found of published times but they would have given some kind of notice of their next intended call since they would not have wanted to cross to Arran — a hazardous and uncertain trip in those days — without ensuring that the maximum number of potential travellers would be waiting to make the crossing. Further, on their inward journeys to the island they would have carried Arran-bound travellers, residents and perhaps a few visitors (who would not have been tourists as such at that time) who wanted to travel to a village other than Lamlash.

Unlike Shillibeer, who chose his own pre-advertised times and decided to which destination he would go, and, indeed, which of several routes he would take, McBride would have had his times of arrival and departure forced upon him by wind, tide and the intentions stated of the sailing boat skippers.— to say nothing of actions made in the face of 'circumstances beyond control'. His route, too, was forced upon him, since there was then, and is now, only one possible way to get from Brodick to Lamlash, unless perhaps one follows the example of the chaps in G. K. Chesterton's poem:

". . . . . *The night we went to Birmingham by way of Beachy Head.*"

As to the fare, I imagine it would have been the same amount per head for Mistress McNee on Wednesday as it had been for Mr. Thompson the day — or week — before.

McBride was the owner of the first cart of its type to be seen in Arran and, for some time, the only cart as well. He may have had his times forced upon him, whereas Shillibeer worked them out scientific-ally; he may have had his route forced upon him, while Shillibeer gave much thought to a combination of many different ways of 'getting there', and it is true that he was able to carry only six or seven people, one-third of the number George Shillibeer could uplift at a time. I will even concede that McBride did not carry a conductor, a personage that no omnibus should be without, according to Shillibeer, and several senior London policemen since then as well. I do put forward the suggestion, however, that McBride, like Barkiss in *David Copperfield* and other country carriers, may have unknowingly anticipated the omnibus which first ran through the streets of London in 1829.

There are no details of McBride's day-to-day activities and, in any case, after less than three years of hiring his 'omnibus' or running it to a schedule, and carrying freight as well, he lost it. This was at sea! The vehicle was shipped for repair to a coachbuilder near to the site on which the present day Ailsa-Volvo omnibus factory stands in Irvine, Ayrshire. But, alas, the ship foundered and was lost with all its cargo, and most of its hands.

A Machrie family — of whom more later — started a coachbuilding business during the ensuing 10 years; they were certainly well-established by 1826, but by that time McBride had either lost heart or was discouraged from starting again by the fast-growing number of wheeled and sprung passenger/freight carts being used in south Arran, and copied nearer Brodick.

Anyway, pre-Shillibeer omnibus operator, or just another early carrier, Mr. McBride was the first Arran resident to carry fare-paying passengers in the island.

HIRERS & DRIVERS

Every bit as important to this story as the Kaspar Ribbecks, Ernest Gordons and 'Col' Curries, are the lesser-known names, of people who, although they did not develop their work to the stage whereby their names were painted on the sides of large omnibus fleets, were nevertheless a keystone in the foundation of Arran's passenger transport system.

COSSIMO LATONA was such a man and we shall be looking at his main activity a little later in this book. A story I heard from several sources seems typical of the man and his contemporaries. Cossimo Latona was a well-known figure in Brodick before the Great War. His services as a guide for Goat Fell were in great demand and, when not engaged in driving parties to, and conducting them over, Goat Fell and other parts of Arran, he dealt in, and with, horses and carriages.

One day, he decided to sell one of his carriage horses and so he took it to the Brodick Fair. Having found a prospective buyer, he clinched the deal, then retired to a bar with one or two of his cronies. While discussing the day's business with the company present, he was interrupted by an agitated chap, the one to whom he had sold the horse for five pounds.

"Mr. Latona" said the chap, "the horse you've sold me has just dropped down dead!"

Cossimo took a pull at his pint, and a sip of his 'hauf' and gave the matter some thought. "Do you tell me that now?" he asked. "It has never done that before!"

JOHN DAVIDSON was probably the first omnibus operator (in the true sense of the word) in Arran. He lived in Brodick and went regularly to Corrie and back with fare-paying passengers from 1870, and at other times took tours and excursions over the String Road. A two-horse charabanc was used, although this was pulled by an extra horse when a trip to Lochranza was run. The vehicle was not constructed as a three-horse machine, so it seems likely that the extra horse was tied behind and only used for the steeper parts of the journey.

Despite competition from Ribbeck and from Currie, who both had mail contracts, to say nothing of a Mr. Bannatyne and others plying for hire in the area, John Davidson seems to have maintained a steady though not spectacular service until his death in 1911.

NEIL McBRIDE was responsible for building the Pier Garage at Brodick in 1923, now part of the Arran Transport & Trading Company's head office and depot. In addition to a fleet of touring cars, McBride also had a FIAT charabanc, a 14-seater, and an Overland interchangeable goods and passenger carriage. He installed petrol pumps, thought to be the first in Arran, and appears to have been the first, and for a long time the only, charabanc operator to keep a motor-coach in a state of constant readiness during the winter against the possibility of a demand for a hire from a large party. He does not seem to have entertained any thoughts of an omnibus service, and sold his interests (less the Overland, which went to Latona) to Finlay Kerr-Newton in 1930.

DONALD CURRIE of Rosaburn, Brodick, had several motor wagonettes for hire during the early 1920s. They may have been used from time to time as taxis but falling as they did midway between a large motor car and a small charabanc, it is likely that Donald Currie would have found it more economic to cater for larger families who wanted a tour or excursion.

JOHN MACKENZIE, to whom reference is made in another chapter, had several very smart horse-drawn carriages which he operated from his home at King's Cross. In addition to the service he operated from time to time for the steamer passengers embarking and disembarking at King's Cross point, or one of the piers, he was a regular traveller to Brodick Fair. Each year he polished his carriages — or rather his son, Ian, did — and off they went to the Fair, expecting to pick up fare-paying passengers along the way. Just as regularly, however, the many Mackenzies and others related to him, were just as determined to go, and most of John's trips to Brodick Fair proved to be family outings in the end!

He thought seriously about obtaining a motor omnibus when Willie Currie of Kilmory decided that SJ424, the light blue Ford wagonette, was not for him, and it might have gone to King's Cross instead of back to Pirnmill. In the end John MacKenzie decided that he was too old to learn to drive it, and that his sons were too young, so the MacKenzie fleet never became motorised, and Johnny Anderson had an 'as new, only one owner, less than 60 miles' second-hand vehicle in stock for a short time.

In my possession I have a book, *No Better Than I Should Be — The Making of a Minister* by the Reverend James Dow, the well-known Lochranza Church of Scotland minister, wit, raconteur and broadcaster. It puts me in mind of an incident which happened, not in the 1920s but the 1970s, when Jimmy Dow used to borrow Duncan MacAllister's minibus to take his parishioners to the church at Lochranza. I lived in Catacol in those days, and was asked by some visitors who were at a nearby house what shops and banks there were in the district. I explained that there were no shops in Catacol but that there was a mobile shop on Mondays, a mobile bank on Tuesdays, a mobile library on Wednesdays, the Calor gas dealer came on Thursdays, another mobile bank on Fridays, and a mobile chemist came on Saturdays. I explained that most of these visiting facilities stopped outside individual houses on request. At that moment, the Reverend James Dow pulled up beside us, in the minibus, near enough fully-robed for the coming service. It never occurred to me until the next day why the people to whom I had been speaking had, quite literally, fallen back in amazement!

To return to the 1900s, no account of the early days of transport in the Isle of Arran would be complete without reference to:

HENDERSON, a Glasgow carriage hirer and funeral director, who was a regular visitor to the island, and who, as early as 1904, noted the number of well-to-do families which came to the island for lengthy periods without transport of their own. He made arrangements with many of them whereby a complete carriage, with horses and a liveried driver, was sent from Glasgow and waiting for them in Arran when they landed. From 1904 to 1907 he found it worth his while to send several carriages and drivers from Glasgow 'on spec' but after that date the local carriage hire trade was beginning to develop.

Omnibus operators such as Donnie Lennox and Finlay Kerr-Newton were at pains to point out to me that it was not just the owners who were responsible for developing the omnibuses and coaches. The drivers worked very hard as well, and stories concerning some of them are still told.

GUNBOAT SMITH came to the island for most of the summers in the years between 1923 and 1939. He drove on a casual basis for Lennox, Gordon, McNeill and other east Arran motor hirers. Some-times he drove a service omnibus but more often than not he was on the tours. He missed only three seasons in the 17 years he was associated with the island. By one of those strange coincidences which happen from time to time, a photograph was taken of him driving a charabanc on tour during one of the summers he did not come to Arran, and the charabanc he was driving came here a few years later, so Gunboat (nobody knows what his real name was) has his photo in this book alongside the chara concerned, although, strictly speaking, neither he nor it should be here, and would not have been if photographs of the charabanc in the island had been available. During winter months he toured the Scottish mainland with a travelling circus as an exhibition boxer — £5 to anyone who can go three rounds with Gunboat Smith!

SILENCE McDOWELL was anything but silent. He was a Lamlash man, a driver who never let anything get him down to the point where he no longer felt like making some sort of music. Usually he whistled, in his omnibus and out of it — a habit for which **Neil Black** was noted 40 years later — and many's the serenade he sang when driving an open-top chara back over the Ross Road at dusk, particularly when there were lady passengers. He must have been a very popular man since, even now, people who remember him do so with a smile.

WEE JOCK MACDONALD, in later years, was one of the shortest of the Arran coach drivers, a distinction that **John Smith** had in the 1970s. Wee Jock drove a Stewart machine and it is said that you could set your watch by him. He was never involved in any accident or scrape, which in itself, Arran roads being what they are, is a remarkable feat.

GRANT WEIR, who died a few years ago, had a reputation for courtesy and patience which was a by-word. His contemporaries described him as one of the safest drivers on Arran, and certainly the most polite. For several years he drove the Ten-A tour and knew a great number of local stories and legends, most of which he passed on to his passengers.

He was driving a coachload of visitors round the island on a tour recently and while on the String Road he started talking about the natural history of the island. A coach driver, if you stop to think about it, has to have the same gift as a politician. An audience of — say — 40 people who, between them, are talking among themselves, sound rather like the Tower of Babel when they found that the damp-proofing course had been left out and take some talking over, but in no time they were all listening to a discourse on the flora and fauna of Arran. The "patter" veered round to the subject of snakes. There are several types of snake in Arran (I exclude the Smooth Snake, since I am given to understand that it is, in fact, a lizard). Grass Snakes are to be found here and there, but the Adder, or Viper, is the most common. The Adder/Viper is poisonous (so don't eat any of them) and is said to grow to a length of 18 inches, although I have seen one nearer 2'6". It was not a grass snake, it was not one following close behind the other like two Glasgow PTE omnibuses, it was one snake, and I don't care what David Attenborough says; Kek Arnott was there and he saw it, too. However, it was nothing like so remarkable as the snake that was drawn to the attention of the tour passengers on the String Road. This, the driver said, was Arran's most exotic snake, black with yellow markings, harmless, and usually to be found on the sunny side of a tarmac slope with its five foot length typically coiled into a figure 6. "In fact," said he, "I can see a fully-grown adult one just down the road." He stopped the coach and invited the passengers to alight and walk forward *quietly and slowly* so that they could see this specimen of *Ferodo Elasticus* in its natural element.

And that is how Grant Weir persuaded 39 tour passengers to get off a coach in the middle of nowhere to look at a broken fan belt.

While I cannot note every single driver, even though they are all very interesting people, I cannot omit the man to whom this book is dedicated:

GEORGE MUNRO is a man with whom I have always got on well, and I am sure that he will not take offence at the story I am going to tell about him.

For the first few years of the 1970s, George, who has been driving omnibuses for 30 years, used an odd-looking Bedford coach for the Brodick – Corrie – Pirnmill run. It was one of those second-hand machines which Arran Transport inherited, and a schoolboy wrote a letter which was published in the local newspaper saying that the vehicle was not fit to keep chickens in. It so happened that the weekend the letter was printed, George had a dispute with a farm tractor — something to do with the right of way, I expect — and the result was that every window on the offside of the omnibus was broken. To keep the machine in service while spare windows were being obtained, a large sheet of plyboard was nailed over the gaps. I boarded the omnibus at Lochranza the following Monday, and surveyed the wood.

"Good idea, George," I said, "that will stop the chickens escaping!"

George was not amused; and after the first mile, I dared not meet his gaze in the mirror, lest I should be shrivelled to ashes where I sat! The omnibus in question was CJS 888.

HAMILTON KERR, who dates from to the 1930s, was a regular Lennox driver. He now lives in Ardrossan but visits Arran twice a year just to keep in touch, although he has been retired for some years. He made several special trips to Arran during 1976, just to give some information for, and sort out one or two matters arising from the notes for this book. For this, and for the photographs of *Silver Bullet* loaded and unloaded shown elsewhere, I am very grateful.

To return to the operators, there were two, early in the motor age, with the same name. Both lived in Lamlash, but were not related.

DUNCAN KERR was the first motor hirer in Lamlash (on the eastern side of Arran, come to that) and had several Ford motor cars for private parties and taxi work. He never advertised a tour, his policy being to make the machines available and take the passengers to wherever they wanted to go. Even so, he always had plenty of suggestions for families and parties who did not know the island well. At some time during the 1920s he sent a car 'on spec' to King's Cross on days when a heavy load was expected from one of the excursion steamers.

JOHN KERR put a GMC wagonette SJ222 on the road in 1918. It ran regularly between Lamlash and King's Cross, with some return trips (in the period 1919–1922) made by way of Whiting Bay first, if a sufficient number of passengers were on hand to justify it. **Mary Cannon** has told me that the GMC was used on more than one occasion to take Lamlash schoolchildren to Dougarie Lodge, between Machrie and Imachar. That was before the road programme of 1929, and the burn flowing down from Glen Iorsa invariably necessitated the unloading of the children, who crossed the burn on stepping-stones, while the GMC negotiated the rather difficult ford there. SJ222 was sold to Ernest Bolt in 1928.

Some of the passengers, too, have passed into legend; there was the chap who went from King's Cross road end to Lamlash or Brodick bars most evenings, and was loaded on to the last Lennox omnibus to Whiting Bay in the evening. The conductress always put him out most carefully at his stop, taking care to lay him gently on to the grass. On more than one summer morning, the crew of the first omnibus from Whiting Bay would see him still lying there sleeping it off. It has been said that he was eventually banned from every public bar and every public omnibus in Arran, and that he used to row to the Carradale Hotel (about five miles across the Kilbrannan Sound), but I record that on the basis that it is an Arran legend, not necessarily a true story.

GREETING KATE was one of Ernest Gordon's favourite characters, and if she is by any freak of nature still alive and reading this, I'd like her to know that Ernest often spoke of her before he died, with affection. She was rarely known to smile, and always addressed herself to her knitting, no matter what was going on around her — singing, jokes in a hall during a mystery tour (she was a regular patron) spectacular scenery, some of the finest views in Scotland (by which, of course, I mean the finest views in the world) — all were one to Greeting Kate. She just sat there and knitted.

Early in the 1930s, a weekly season ticket was made available on Lennox and Gordon omnibuses. In line with the joint working agreement of both services, the season tickets were accepted on either service, no matter which one of the two had issued it. The price was five shillings (25p) and although they were intended for *bona fide* workers, i.e., people travelling between any two points between Brodick and Whiting Bay once each way on six days in any week, they could be used, according to the terms on which they were issued, for as many journeys between Brodick and Whiting Bay, from the 0530 runout in the morning of Monday to the last one in at 2300 on Saturday night. (There were no Sunday omnibus services in those days).

Kate purchased a ticket from Gordon's at Lamlash, and immediately after breakfast she boarded a Lennox omnibus and knitted. She got off at around lunch time, then after a short nap went in search of an omnibus. All afternoon the omnibus went back and forth between Whiting Bay and Brodick. So did Kate and her knitting. A short break for tea, when Kate got off by a tearoom at Lamlash, and back on the same vehicle as it returned. There she stayed until gone 2130. By tea time on the Saturday Kate had clocked-up 800 miles, according to 'Pa' Lennox, whose main objection, not unnaturally, was that while it was one of his omnibuses she was riding on, the ticket (and therefore the five shillings she had paid for it) were Gordon's!

The following week, Ernest Gordon kept an eye on the situation, and confirmed at the end of it that Kate (who had purchased a season for the second week) had travelled about 800 miles. He also told 'Pa' Lennox that she had knitted three sweaters, a scarf, two cardigans and a pair of bedsocks. At the end of that week her holiday was over, and back she went to the mainland for another year. During her 50-week absence, the conditions of carriage appertaining to weekly season tickets were altered to exclude all but *bona fide* workers.

Greeting Kate had a sister who travelled with her at all times, including the mystery tours, and during the record-breaking season-ticket runs. The sister died in the mid-1930s, but Kate still came to Arran. She is remembered as a reserved but kindly lady, not much given to speaking unless spoken to first, when she was friendly in her replies, even to strangers. As a regular on Gordon's and Lennox tours, she was well-known, much-liked and sadly missed when, after the end of the Second German War, she failed to return for her annual holiday.

Then there was a dog ...... that used to travel from Corrie to Machrie, changing at Lochranza to do its courting. (I am only telling you what several of the older residents of Lochranza have told me!). It seems that the dog used to hop on to a North Arran Motors vehicle at various places between Brodick and Sannox, get off and wander over to a Weir or Robertson omnibus on which it sat until it got to Machrie, at which point it followed other passengers off the vehicle. Nobody ever saw it go back, but it was seen to make the outward journey many times in the mid-1940s.

THOMAS LANKESTER of the Lamlash Hotel had a 16-seat Dodge. It was registered to him — SJ378 — in 1923 for use as a 'hire' vehicle, although it was used only to transport hotel guests to and from the Lamlash Pier, and for excursions of hotel guests during the 1923 season. In 1924 and 1925 it was available for private hire to anyone in the island, and 'Silence' (Donald) and his brother John McDowell were the regular drivers of this, and a touring car also kept by the hotel. **Mary Hodge,** the daughter of Thomas Lankester, tells me that it was never used as an omnibus — she also recalled hanging on behind Hamilton's brake in the late 1900s, and at least until 1912. This was a regular game played by the children at Lagg, where she lived at the time, and it seems that skinned knees were the order of the day more often than not. The game — as I understand it — was to hang on to the back of the brake without putting a foot to the ground *and* without being discovered by the driver. Last one to fall off, or let go, was the winner.

JESSIE MARY BANNATYNE of Millhead, Lamlash also had several motor vehicles for hire. The first of these was SJ362, a Dodge. According to a list I was given, it was a charabanc with 15 seats, against which several people who remember it say that it was a touring car. Jessie Bannatyne was a Guide Captain at that time and Sal Bannatyne who was in her troop and often rode in it, says that it was a 'big ugly thing painted blue, but definitely not a chara'. It was registered in 1922. In 1926 a royal blue six–seat Ford touring car either replaced it or joined it. This was SJ552, a very powerful left-hand drive machine which, like the Dodge, was driven and maintained by the McDowell brothers.

On the subject of hires, one of the most remarkable — and certainly the most unexpected — took place well before the motor age had come to Arran, and necessitated the carriage of more than 100 people from south Arran. This was in August of 1899, when the North British Railway Company's paddlesteamer *Redgauntlet* — a regular vessel on the weekly round-Arran run — came a little too close to a reef off the shore near Sliddery. She was holed, and had to be beached. I should, perhaps, stress that in this particular case, the expression 'hire' is not only incorrect, but unjust as well, since the local people were of great help and comfort to the passengers. Many local men waded out to assist the ship's boats (which were of inadequate number on all passenger ships until after 1912) and several of them risked their lives bringing people ashore. Once ashore, the passengers were taken to Whiting Bay in all kinds of vehicles, farm carts and wagons, as well as passenger vehicles, after being dried-out and given hospitality in local houses. There was no loss of life; indeed, the only significant loss seems to have been of the captain's position, since although the Board of Trade did not suggest it, the company reduced him('dipped' him, as I believe mariners say) to first officer.

This, in turn, brings us to accidents, of which there are very few on record, at least, so far as Arran's omnibuses and tour cars are concerned. I have heard a tale from several sources of a Talbot tour car missing a bend on the Heights (that is the section of the Lamlash to Whiting Bay road where it leaves Lamlash and hairpins round to climb over Cordon on the way to the south). It appears that the car made two — some authorities say three — complete somersaults, during which time several people fell through the canvas roof, and after which they and the car landed on the beach. Incredibly, and I use the word in its broadest possible sense, nobody was hurt.

Another accident took place where the road from Brodick descends into Lamlash just before the right-hand bend, where the road follows the shore. A brand new Lennox 20–seat FIAT saloon coach was descending and the brakes failed. The driver was reluctant to take the bend at the bottom at any great speed, and to keep going was out of the question, since the tide was in, and he did not want to get the vehicle wet. So he drove the vehicle into the bank at the side of the road, and this stopped it. Unfortunately, it became jammed, and it was not possible to open the passenger (and only) door. Emergency doors were unheard of in those days, R.T.A. part 4 and the Motor Vehicles (Construction & Use) Regulations were a long way into the future. So there it sat, until it could be pulled out of the bank and the passengers — all of whom were unhurt — could be let out.

The 1920s were a colourful and adventurous decade for tourists in Arran. Although the motor age had arrived with a bang, the roads were not ready for it, and no tour car or charabanc trip could be guaranteed to be uneventful. Punctures were common and many drivers spent their tea-breaks mending holes in the tyres, usually in one of the many burns in the island. It was fortunate for us, one driver told me, "that you cannot go very long in Arran without passing water"!

The Brodick to Whiting Bay road through Lamlash was the busiest during this decade, and subsequent ones; a survey carried-out in 1972–73 found that it was the busiest road in any of the Clyde islands. By the end of the 1920s this section of the coast road was adequately surfaced and, in addition to charabanc and motor car tours using it, there was an omnibus through Lamlash in each direction every 20 minutes, operated by the Lennox and Gordon companies, of whom more later. It could well have been said of them, as it was said of Hillman's coaches in Brentwood, Essex, that "there is always one in sight".

IAN MARTIN, now living at Ardrossan, sent me a photograph, taken in 1932, of some omnibuses being washed in Monamore burn at Lamlash during a water shortage when the use of hoses was restricted. This was just one of the facets of the life of a charabanc or omnibus driver in Arran in those days; long hours, with a bit of painting, panel beating, tyre repair, oil drum unloading, minor maintenance and cleaning the vehicles as well as attending to the requirements of passengers who had mislaid their luggage or forgotten what time to be back at the vehicle after a tea stop.

THE LAIRD OF LAGG. This is not the nickname given to a local omnibus or coach driver. Indeed, for such an intensive scene as transport, there seem to be very few nicknames — I've known small mainland depots with more of them at any one time than Arran has coined in a century. So far as the vehicles go, there was only 'Campbeltown Kate', 'The Train', and a modern Bedford known by just a few of today's omnibus drivers as 'The Queen Mary' (CSJ200M Arran Transport). As to the drivers themselves, names were shortened, of course, to 'Hammie', 'Phil', and the like, but the only nicknames I have come across are 'Silence' McDowell, 'Cappie' MacBride, 'Biffo' Munro, (Sorry, George, but most people *did* know that already!), and 'Chuecter' Nicholson.

  To return to the Laird of Lagg, he does not really belong in this book, since the coach he was driving was not plying for hire and anyway belongs in the 16th or 17th century, when the Laird was thought to have pledged his soul to the devil (a thing many people still do today). One very wild, wet and windy winter night (you cannot have a ghost story starting on a calm summer afternoon) he was driving his coach at a great rate along the track, and straight into Sliddery Water, either because he missed the bridge, or because it

collapsed under him. Anyway, Laird, coach and horses, in they all
went, and the Laird was drowned. His ghost is said to haunt that
stretch of track over which the Ross Road has since been built.

ALASTAIR MACBRIDE, referred to as 'Cappie', is, at the time of
writing, the regular driver of Arran Coaches No.845. He is descended
from the 'original' McBride described in the first chapter, and the son
of the 'Brodick Pier Garage' McBride mentioned elsewhere. The
different spelling (Mc & Mac) is due to a registrar's mistake. It seems
that when the infant Alastair was brought to the attention of the
Registrar for Births, Deaths and Marriages, the said Registrar started
to write 'Alistair' and was told: "It is spelt with an A". The Registrar
assumed that this referred to the 'Mac' and spelt it accordingly. He was
then told that the first name was spelt with an A and in the confusion,
he altered it to Alastair, but forgot to change the Mac back to Mc.

Where Danny Stewart and Donny Campbell are more 'lively' in
appearance, and while Bruce Hough is always seen with a smile on his
face, Alastair MacBride has a very measured, reserved way of
speaking, and a straight-face delivery, as the stage comedians say. It
follows, therefore, that any joke he makes is all the funnier for being
completely unexpected. One such joke was pulled on me. The coach
was sitting out of service at Blackwaterfoot, and I was sitting in it
talking to Alastair. I noticed a stout black thread running up the right-
hand edge of the windscreen. This I assumed to be be one of those
home-made devices used by coach drivers the world over to enable
them to undo the left-hand catch over the destination screen trap
without getting up from the driving seat. I asked Alastair what it was,
and instead of telling me, he told me — what everyone in Arran knows
— that just up the road from where we were sitting were the King's
Caves, where Robert the Bruce is said to have watched the spider.

"Of course," he said, "it might not have been these caves, but there
are a lot of spiders about."

So saying, he pulled the thread, and a large black plastic spider
appeared from behind the interior mirror and ran down the windscreen!

Of such stuff are coach drivers made!

DANNY STEWART gave a great deal of amusement to some of his passengers in the late 1970s when he turned up for a tour in a bright ginger, shoulder-length curly wig — they would be just amused to know that while removing his gear and effects from No.400 and transferring them to the newly-arrived (and allocated to him) 139, he forgot where he was and stepped back from the driving seat of the new coach on to a step which was not there. Mind you, he didn't miss any more steps — he bounced off every one of them on to the tarmac! He was off sick for a time, and no doubt time has healed to the extent that he can see the funny side of it now — just as the rest of us did then.

PHIL BROOMHEAD had been in Arran for about a year and had been driving omnibuses for rather less time than that by the time he had built up a reputation for service to the extent that arrangements could be made for a package "to be given to the Pirnmill driver and dropped off". It was a couple of shirts for a fancy dress party one way, and a bottle of medicine the other; in both cases Phil was the last to hear of the arrangement, but fell in with it readily.

GEORGE MACGREGOR, (back to the 1930s again, but it serves to keep the reader on his/her toes) was a regular visitor to Arran and something of a poet. The poem reproduced on page 39 will show how he felt about Arran. It will also be noted that coach tours in the 1932–34 period passed along the Kildonan to Whiting Bay road, over which no omnibus rolled on Sundays; and that a 1415 departure for the all-Arran trip was normal. (I suspect poetic licence in the 'Sunday' and '2:15' but anyway, let Mr. MacGregor tell it).

MYSTERY TOURS, as mentioned elsewhere, were of a type peculiar only to Arran since, as far as I know, the only other transport system bound so tightly into a circle is the Glasgow subway. Mainland mystery tours are a different matter, of course, and I can recall seeing them advertised on blackboards propped against coaches at Southend in Essex, in Torquay and in London. Places like those have literally hundreds of routes to choose from, leading to hundreds of destinations. I recall the joke — maybe you do, too — about the chap who went on a mystery tour from Bournemouth every day for a week. The driver used to suggest a 'pool' with each person putting in five shillings and the name of the place they guessed the vehicle would be going. The chap in question was most impressed with the lucky streak the coach driver was on to —he'd guessed right, and won all the money six days in a row!

A story is told of an Arran 'busman — his name is given, but not in this book — who took a holiday towards the end of the season, and went to stay for a fortnight in an English seaside town. A local shipping company was offering mystery tours of three days' duration, and our hero decided to join the tour, more or less on the spur of the moment.

That night he'd retired to bed in his cabin, and was woken by the steward next morning with a cup of tea. He looked out of his cabin porthole, and saw his local Arran pier, with his coaches all lined up ready to take him on Stage 2 of the mystery tour!

There are plenty of stories of Arran drivers and their passengers, some best left unrepeated, for now, but I am sure no offence will be taken by the participants in an incident many years ago, when a conductress felt obliged to put a passenger — her brother — off the omnibus because, although not offensively so, he was drunk. Off he got, somewhat bewildered, no doubt, at this unexpected firmness on the part of his sister, and as the omnibus pulled away, he fell against the side of it, and under the back wheel. Although he did not sustain any serious injury, he was unable to get up again owing to a fractured thigh, and the omnibus from which he had been ejected passed him several times before the conductress realised that his horizontal position was not entirely due to the juice of the barley!

Visitors to Arran's west will have noticed the posting box at the junction of the String road and Machrie Moor road end. It is set in a stone beehive-shaped structure, with some strange-looking marks chiselled upon it. These are stone-mason's marks, applied solely for decoration, although when asked what they meant a Postbus driver recently told one of his passengers that it was "Ancient Gaelic for 'Post Early for Christmas'."!

The Rev. David McHutcheson, now retired and living in Lauder, told me several tales which I found most amusing. One of these concerned a local omnibus which had its axles out of alignment. It was known locally as 'The Crab' by virtue of its sideways motion along the

She says to me: "You're working sore
To keep the wolf away,
If once we had a little more
We'd take a holiday."

Says I: "My dear, you do your share
At makin' both ends meet;
We have enough to pay our fare,
The morn we'll have a treat.

"The coast of Arran we'll explore
By 'bus we'll take a run."
We couldn't wish for any more,
And, oh! It was such fun!

We started off at 2.15,
And drove right up through Corrie,
Enjoying fine the lovely scene
And not the least bit sorry.

And then we passed thro' Sannox Glen,
Where dust o' Barytes shines;
The road takes many a twist and bend
Just by the Barytes mines.

We carried on o'er mountains steep,
The driver knew no fear;
On either side were flocks of sheep
And many a herd of deer.

The next wee town that came in sight
As we went driving on
Was dear Lochranza, nice and bright,
Land of the setting sun.

Then Catacol, so nice and trig,
With whitewashed walls so neat,
Altho' it is not very big
It's got its own main street.

We breasted then another hill,
And oh! the 'bus did travel,
He took us right onto Pirnmill
With its lovely beach of gravel.

Past Dougarie and Machrie Bay,
Auchnagallon and Tormore,
And came in sight of Shiskine gay,
Then out down to the shore.

Down thro' Torbeg, Blackwaterfoot,
Then headed straight for Lagg;
We'd climb a hill, then down would shoot
O'er hill and dale and crag.

We passed thro' Lagg so nicely set
In such a cosy dip;
But to get out he had to let
His engine fairly rip.

Then at Kildonan we got tea
Near by the Pladda light,
Where coast of Ireland you can see
Just if the day be bright.

We finished tea, then off we set
And passed thro' Whiting Bay.
That Sunday trip we shan't forget —
It was a lovely day!

We made our way home thro' Lamlash,
And saw the Holy Isle;
We never grudged our bit of cash;
For it was well worthwhile.

At six o'clock we landed home,
Nor felt a bit the worse,
And glad to say we still had some
More coppers in the purse.

To anyone on pleasure bent
I now pass on this tip;
No money could be better spent
Than on a Sunday trip.

From: **'Day Trip to Arran'**
George D. MacGregor

road and, when motorists met it on a bend, the drill was to stop and
give it as much room as possible because, with the wheels pointing one
way, the nose pointing another, and its wall-eyed driver looking in yet
a third direction, it was difficult to estimate what path it would
actually take.Is there so much difference between Peshawar and
Pirnmill? Although it was going up the Khyber Pass and not down the
Kildonan low road it might once have been an Arran omnibus. It was,
after all, an ancient Bedford that had worked in Scotland. Scots
machines and Scots people do go all over the world, even though some
of them do resent other people doing the same thing by coming to live
in Scotland. With such an omnibus George Munro could have
necessitated the widening of the North Glen Sannox road, Hammy
Kerr would have loved it, and Gordons' Motors mystery tours could
have had just one more facet to their operation.

   To return to Arran. On his first trip here as a small boy the minister
told me that rain had been about the Clyde all day. However, his
family had managed to reach St. Enoch station without getting wet
and, on the trip to Arran, they were well to the fore of the rush for cover
which is always attendant upon rain falling on a Clyde steamer. By the
time they got to Whiting Bay the rain had cleared. The Lennox driver
booked to meet them with *The Silver Bullet* suggested that as the rain
had cleared they might like the sidescreens down. (Younger readers
may care to note that in those days there were no such things as
Triplex wind-down windows — nominally transparent fabric was
affixed to the sides of drophead cars by means of studs) The
McHutcheson family agreed that, as it was a fine day, they could
dispense with the sidescreens, although the hood was left up against
the possibility — one might even say the probability — of a brew up
from the radiator. The place to which they were going, a remote farm,
was down a side lane bordered by two hedges which, owing to the
Arran climate and the length of time since they were last cut, nearly
met in the middle of the road. They were sopping wet with rain and by
the time the car had squeezed past them to the farm the family were as
wet as if they had been caught in the storm. It was, as the minister told
me, his first experience of Arran and endeared him to the place so
much that he has come back many times and intends to do so again.

DONNY CAMPBELL was, literally, button-holed by one visitor, who interrupted a conversation with another passenger that Donny was having on Brodick Pier.

"Hey youse," said the visitor, "Is this Blackwaterfoot?" At the same time as he barked out this question he nodded over Donny's shoulder at an omnibus which was clearly marked "Blackwaterfoot".

Donny thought for a minute, then said: "No, this is Brodick. But, (he paused) if you get on the bus it will take you to Blackwaterfoot."

ROBERT SILLARS, who lived at the top of the Knowe Road in Brodick, started hiring Victorias and wagonettes in 1907. They were available for long periods and for excursions, but he preferred to use them for short-distance work, when given the choice. By the time he wound up his business in 1925, he was in partnership with his son, Neil, and the fleet included several motor cars, although the horse-drawn vehicles outnumbered them by about three to one. A well-known Brodick resident, who has asked me not to name him, remembers getting a hiding when, as a young lad in 1924, he accidentally let the brake off on a wagonette he was cleaning. He tells me that it wasn't the run down the hill which damaged the vehicle — the sudden stop at the foot of the hill was responsible for that!

By the mid-1920s there were, literally, hundreds of people flocking to Arran on afternoon cruises 'Doon the Watter', in addition to the visitors who had come for a week or so. Local people were quick to cater for them, and many motor taxis were licenced. Among them were M. & J. Currie of Brodick, who ran a shop which still bears their name. In 1919 they obtained a black Ford six–seater, SJ209, and in 1924 a similar machine, grey, SJ441. Donald McLardy at Lamlash put a five–seat Ford on the road in 1920, SJ246, and in Whiting Bay Daniel Murray and a Mr. McKirdy had entered the lists with Ford five–seaters in competition with each other, and everyone else in Whiting Bay by 1922. The cars were SJ345 and SJ328. In Corriecravie, John Mulholland put SJ400, another five–seat Ford on the road in 1923. These, of course, are just a few of the many people who catered for the visitors in the 1920s. Another one was Colin Currie of Brodick — he lived in Douglas Row and was not a close relation of Col Currie at Shiskine. To him we find a Ford SJ298 registered as a five–seater in

1924. The vehicle in question dates back a few years before that and was purchased by Mr. Currie second-hand.

All of these people contributed something to the development of the tourist industry in the island, and it should be borne in mind that so far as Arran was concerned, the motor car was still very much in its infancy. Even while it was finding its feet in the 1920s there were still developments being tried with horse-drawn vehicles. For instance, John Mackenzie, of King's Cross to Brodick Fair family outing fame, tried the first solid rubber tyres to be fitted to an Arran carriage, and also had the first pneumatic tyres fitted to that kind of vehicle at the same time that Kaspar Ribbeck was taking a chance on the rather primitive pneumatics available to motor vehicles, which goes to show that MacKenzie still had faith in the future of the horse-drawn vehicle.

The free-for-all competition eventually settled down to a regulated, but nevertheless colourful, industry, and since the purpose of this book is to examine that industry, it would be as well to start now.

Before doing so, I must make reference to one distinguished omnibus operator — no less a person than Walter Alexander, the Falkirk omnibus pioneer whose name is still used when talking of the Midland, Fife and Northern Scottish Bus Group fleets. It is said that he often took a holiday in Arran, and on more than one occasion expressed an interest during the 1920s and early 1930s in acquiring an omnibus service here. Needless to say, he did not do so — perhaps even he knew competition when he saw it!

ARRAN AND THE ALBION. Copies of the photograph on Plate 19 are to be found in many bars and public rooms in the island, as well as in a local history book. The car in the photograph is said to be an Albion, although in fact this is not so. It is a Panhard & Levassor.

It was purchased by Mr. N. O. Fulton for experimental purposes. It is seen here just outside Brodick, in 1896, with Mr. Fulton driving and various other members of the Fulton family seated in the machine. Incorrectly, local legend has it that the car was the property of a local Arran family, the Fullartons, but this is not so. The car belonged to Mr. N. O. Fulton. It was the first motor car ever to come to Arran, and a brief account of its crossing from the mainland will not come amiss here. The purser of the G.& S.W.R. steamer *Jupiter* had never seen a motor-carriage before and it most certainly was not covered by the fare-tables carried on Clyde steamers of the day. However, nothing put a Clyde steamer purser off his balance; there is a story, for instance, of a Caledonian Steam Packet Company official who had to leaf right through his rule-and-fare book in order to find guidance on what to charge for a family pet which was carried by a member of a party travelling to the island.

'According to my book,' he said, 'horses are charged the same as cows, and goats count as sheep, but that there tortoise is an insect!'

The purser of the *Jupiter* and Mr. Fulton discussed the matter and, in the end, one pound changed hands. Included in the party were Mr. and Mrs. Hugh Fulton, an aunt, as well as Mr. T. Blackwood Murray and Mr. G. Johnston — rather more than the motor-carriage could carry. Just how this photograph came to be taken is not known, but the "family afternoon run" as shown here would not have been repeated often since the whole point of bringing the vehicle to the island was for Messrs. Fulton, Blackwood Murray and Johnston to carry out a series of trials and experiments with it. Speed, endurance and economy tests were carried out'round the island', although I think it likely that the route was over the String road and round through Kilmory rather than right up round Lochranza, since the road north of Sannox was still rather primitive, even by pre-1900 Arran standards. Several days were spent on the hills of the String, and when the hill-climbing capabilities had been assessed a series of trials between Brodick and Sannox were carried out.

At the end of the summer of 1896 the motor-carriage left the island. No planks from pier to deck in those days, a block and tackle was used to hoist the machine over the rail and the party went home at the same time. While in Arran the three men decided that their object had been achieved, e.g. to learn from their study of the Panhard and to see if their experiences with it in Arran would give them enough know-how to build cars of their own. We make take it that this was the case since Mr. Johnston went on to found the Arrol-Johnston car factory while Messrs. Fulton and Blackwood Murray opened a factory as well. They called theirs 'Albion Motors'.

CURRIE, Shiskine
Blackwaterfoot — Shiskine — Brodick Village — Brodick Pier

By all accounts, Colin Currie was as colourful a character as you'll find anywhere in Arran. By the turn of the 20th century he was a regular sight on the String road, and his reliability with the mail was a well-established fact. In addition to his farming interests, 'Col' Currie was a postman: he took over the three-days- a-week mail contract from his father, John, and not content with that, he became a postman at the age of 17 in 1886. The horse-drawn brake he used to carry the mail was also available to passengers in and after 1890. The fare, return, between Shiskine and Brodick was two shillings (10p). The service was extended to Blackwaterfoot in 1893, when a sub post office was opened there.

An interesting story is told of how the Arran mailcarts became omnibuses. The story is that Col, and other mailcart contractors, had been in the habit of carrying fare-paying passengers unofficially for some years prior to 1890. In that year, Col and others advised the GPO that the increase in the cost of keeping horses compelled them to ask for an increase in the amount paid for carrying the mail. The GPO (who, no doubt, were aware of the passengers carried to date) replied that no funds were available for this purpose, but that so long as certain precautions were taken, "... might we suggest that you take passengers? Monies received from them in respect of fares paid for the journey taken could then be used by you to defray the extra cost of which you advise us."!

The first departure of the day from Shiskine was at 0530, to meet a steamer due in at Brodick by 0730. It seems likely that a second journey was made, but this may not have been every day. In any case,

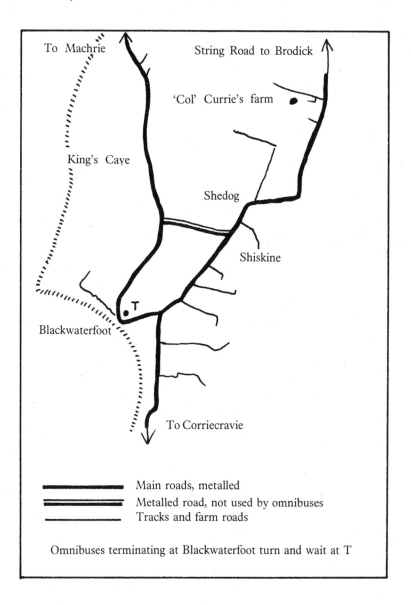

To Machrie

String Road to Brodick

'Col' Currie's farm

King's Cave

Shedog

Shiskine

T

Blackwaterfoot

To Corriecravie

Main roads, metalled
Metalled road, not used by omnibuses
Tracks and farm roads

Omnibuses terminating at Blackwaterfoot turn and wait at T

there was a second journey after 1909. Having boarded the omnibus, all of the passengers would have had to alight after a mile and walk to the top of the hill, a distance of a mile and a half in which the String road climbs to 768 feet above sea level. From this point it drops to 400 feet in less than three-quarters of a mile, after which the descent is not so steep.

To cope with the downward slope, Col had a long wooden handle with a block — also of wood — at one end. This was affixed to the vehicle in such a way that when it was pulled the block was forced against the rim of the wheel, thus slowing down the vehicle. Nothing strange about that, one might think, but Col used to slip a worn-out boot or shoe over the wooden block to save wear and tear. By 1895 local people had got into the habit of leaving their old shoes outside the stable at Shedog, Shiskine, for him to use, and by 1900 the pile of discarded footwear was a landmark, and remained so for the next two decades.

Col rarely went to Brodick himself after the summer of 1905, but always made a point of speaking to the driver of the brake on one pretext or other both before and after each journey to and from Brodick so that he could count the passengers (even though Kaspar Ribbeck had introduced omnibus tickets to the island in 1900, Col had no time for them). A photograph was taken in 1908 just as the brake arrived at Shiskine from Brodick, and shows that Col has found something to discuss with the driver and is in a hurry to get to the brake before the passengers alight and disperse. The brake driver was a man named Archie Robertson, noted for a rhyme he used to declaim when asked if there was any room in the brake,

> *"I've one in the boot and one on the top,*
> *One on the axle and one in the lock,*
> *Are you coming with me, or will you walk?"*

Not exactly the stuff of which Poets Laureate are made, perhaps, but the couplet was every bit as regular — and anticipated — as George Munro's 'Pay'ner gerroff' was for two decades fifty years on.

One of Col's many maxims was "The man who carries the packman carries the pack". From time to time, there was a great deal of competition for passengers at Brodick pier, from carriers who were less regular than those whose names have survived to be recorded in this book. On several occasions passengers were enticed into the vehicles of Col's competitors, and for want of space in those vehicles their luggage was deposited into Colin Currie's brake. As he was otherwise engaged with mail and the luggage of departing passengers, Colin Currie was unable to prevent other drivers using his brake as a luggage tender, but matters were soon put right when he returned to find the seats piled high with trunks and cases. These were un-ceremoniously ejected in the general direction of the offending driver with the words "The man who carries the packman carries the pack" being hurled after the luggage. After 1905, it is likely that Archie Robertson had the same attitude, since Col would certainly have instilled 'company policy' into his staff.

By 1913 Colin Currie arranged for the purchase of a motor charabanc. It was a grey, chain-driven Albion, the first motor omnibus ever to be seen in the island. The story is that Col went to the Albion Motor Works at Scotstoun, Glasgow, in person, at one stage in the proceedings, and was asked how he wanted to pay for the machine. No doubt the question was well wrapped-up in a request for advice on what kind of hire purchase terms he wanted; Albion sales staff were not noted for their rudeness, even to someone as casually dressed as Colin Currie was said to be. Without a word, Col pulled a wad of banknotes from his pocket and peeled off the amount required. This has, of course, passed into legend, and the sum is given as between £600 and £700, depending on where one hears the story, but Mr. Colin A. Currie of Shiskine, a direct descendant of the hero of this tale, has been kind enough to make the family records available to me, and the records state that the price was £650 cash. A photograph of the Albion appears with an incorrect caption 'A Kilmory Coach in Service' in an otherwise accurate history of Arran's villages. In fact, the photograph shown was taken at Col's farm, Ballymichael, a mile in the Brodick direction from Shiskine.

The story of how the photograph came to be taken in the farmyard is amusing. John Robertson, a son of Archie, had been sent to Glasgow to learn to drive and maintain the new Albion, which was driven over the String road with great ceremony — and with Col in the front passenger seat. On arrival at Shiskine, it was found that the stable allocated to garage the vehicle was too small. Nobody knows if this was a great disappointment to Col or not; with no apparent trace of discomfort, he invited people in the crowd which had gathered to find seats in the vehicle, and then directed John Robertson to drive them to his house. The Albion was garaged there for the next fifteen months, and it is there that the photograph was taken, in 1913.

At the end of October, 1914 the Albion charabanc was 'called-up' for military service. Unlike the London General omnibuses, the Currie Albion did not get any nearer to Ypres than Stirling Castle, and spent its war years as a troop carrier. It was seen off with mixed feelings. Aside from the fears and hopes of its passengers on the military journey (to say nothing of the fears and hopes of those who remained behind) it was not universally popular with passengers between Brodick and Blackwaterfoot during 1913 and 1914. You will remember the boots and shoes in the pile outside the Shedog stables? Many people were very wary of the mechanical braking system, and long after it had been explained to them they continued to leave their old boots and shoes on the pile! Even so, as one of them once told me, it was pleasant not to have to walk up the String!

Colin Currie had retired from the Post Office in 1913. He was presented with a handsome chain and seal on which was engraved:

Presented to Colin Currie in recognition of
faithful service as postman in Shiskine
for 47 years
1866 — 1913

The suspension of the 'Motor Omnibus Age' did not last for the entire period of the Great War, at least, not so far as Col was concerned. A green Albion was found in 1915 to replace the one taken by the military and this was used turn and turn about with a horse-brake on the omnibus run. Tours, of course, had been discontinued at the start of the war. A passenger asked Col why the motor omnibus was off the road, and was told that it was due to the shortage of petrol.

"Why don't you mix it with water to make it go further?" she asked.

On the 28th August, 1918 a blue four–seat Ford touring car, SJ186, was added to the fleet, followed by a similar machine in black, SJ211, the following year. Also in 1919 was added SJ288, a 15–seat Albion charabanc.

Tours started to pick up again at the end of the Great War, but Col never saw his fleet at its busiest; he died in 1919, although the eight–seat blue Ford touring car SJ237 that joined the fleet in 1920, after John, the son of Col, had taken over, was registered in February, 1920 to Colin Currie.

In 1921, SJ308, a Ford 16–seat omnibus, painted grey, took the place of the wartime green Albion (the fate of the first vehicle is not remembered), and alternated between tours and the service run with SJ288. SJ347, a blue Ford five–seat touring car, was purchased and registered in 1922 then the firm seemed to settle down to a busy, but nevertheless unexpanding routine with a regular motor omnibus service all the year round, and an augmented omnibus service; charabanc tours, and car hire in the summers until 1925 when SJ446, another Ford charabanc with 14 seats (ordered and registered at the back end of the previous year) came on the scene, followed almost at once by SJ371, a grey five–seat Ford car, SJ402, a black four–seat Ford, SJ480, a six–seat Ford, finished in blue, and SJ472, a grey 14–seat Albion charabanc, of which more later. At the end of the year 1925 SJ500, a green Buick six–seat touring car was registered to John Currie, and this raises an interesting point.

SJ is, or was during most of the period covered by this book, the registration mark used by the Bute County Council. So far as I know, it was issued in consecutive order (wonder who got SJ1?) to motor vehicles purchased new by residents of Buteshire, which comprised the Islands of Bute, Cumbrae and Arran as far as motor-bearing roads went. By 1925 there were apparently only 500 new vehicles registered. Even assuming a fair number of second-hand imports, it seems that there were fewer cars per head of the population in the Clyde islands than elsewhere. The number SJ1340 was reached by 1950, and I am assuming that it was reached on the same basis. Then, after the introduction of the roll-on roll-off car ferry, the number of motor vehicles per head of the population grew larger in the Clyde islands than elsewhere.

To return to Currie's activities, however, the years after 1925 were boom years for the tourist trade. John Currie was one of the people

x   1884 advertisement

BRODICK TO SHISKEN,
BLACKWATER FOOT, & MACHRIE BAY.

From 1st June till end of September Conveyance leaves Shisken Daily to join with 7.10 a.m. Steamer from Brodick; returning on arrival of Steamer connecting with 8.40 a.m. Train from Glasgow (St. Enoch).

Extra on Fridays, in connection with 4.30 p.m. Train from Glasgow; and on Saturdays, with 1.25 and 6.15 p.m. Trains.

Extra accommodation during July and August.

Conveyance from Shisken Daily about 11 a.m.; returning on arrival of Steamers "Guinevere" and "Ivanhoe."

Daily (except Saturdays) from Shisken about 4 p.m.; returning on arrival of Steamer connecting with 4.30 p.m. Train from Glasgow (St. Enoch).

CONVEYANCES KEPT FOR HIRE.

COLIN CURRIE,
SHEDOG, SHISKEN.

saw that scenery was all very well, but that the island would benefit as a whole if tourists could get a bit closer to it than the deck of a steamboat. 'Currie's conveyance' had been included in railway steamer timetables since 1897, and by 1911 a note in a commercial directory indicated that a trip to Shisken (*sic*) could be arranged for trippers doon the watter who did not want to go on for a trip around Ailsa Craig and back. By 1925 John Currie had an arrangement with the London, Midland & Scottish Railway Company for a Central Arran tour over the String road to Blackwaterfoot, down to Sliddery, over the Ross Road to Lamlash, then back to Brodick. The London, Midland & Scottish Railway had been formed in 1923, as a result of an Act of 1921, when experience of railway operation during the Great War, and other circumstances which arose afterwards, dictated the grouping into four of most of Britain's railways. As far as the LMSR was concerned, it was formed to take over and amalgamate the Midland; the London, Tilbury & Southend; the London & North Western; the Lancashire & Yorkshire; the Furness; the Maryport & Carlisle; the Glasgow & South Western, and (six months later than the others) the Caledonian railway companies, including all river and coastal steamer interests. There were one or two other railways scooped-up as well, including a part-interest in the Somerset and Dorset Joint Railway — and the point of this apparent digression is to indicate that Currie's tours (and, of course, others in Arran) were advertised in many parts of western mainland Scotland and most of England as well, by a company which was, in terms of both fully-paid-up share capital and assets, the largest commercial company in the British Empire. It had the greatest number of carriages of the four railway companies, and more public buildings as well, in which it advertised 'places served', even if they were served 'once removed' by people like John Currie.

Of course, the LMSR had arrangements with other Arran operators, so did the London & North Eastern Railway, formed at the same time to take over such railways (and their shipping interests) as the Great Eastern, Great Central, Great Northern, North Eastern, North British and West Highland, so it is likely that Currie had people from all over Britain in his touring charabancs and on his omnibus, since they, too, were active in the early years of their existence. In the absence of an organised Tourist Board in those days it is impossible to state how many people came to the island in the 1920s and 1930s, let alone where they came from, but there were times when Currie's Motors — as they had become — had to re-hire from J. S. Bannatyne and his successor, the MacRae brothers, to cope with the demand for seats.

In 1926 a regular tour of North Arran was introduced. The 14–seat Dodge SJ472 was used for this at first. There is a photograph of it at Corrie in that year (Plate 24), and it is said that on its first trip beyond Sannox it fell through the road! If true, it would indicate that it was much heavier than the average charabanc of the day, since Ribbeck and others had been sending motor charabancs over that road for some time. At any rate the road, which in 1925 seems to have been tar and stone chips laid almost directly on top of bare earth from which the heather had been cleared, gave way, and John Robertson (who is the earliest recorded motor omnibus driver in Arran) had to arrange for a fleet of cars to take on his passengers, and a horse or two to pull out his machine. In addition to any Currie machines which happened to be spare at the time, John Robertson may well have contacted Peter Jenkins at the Hamilton Arms to arrange for his grey Ford six–seater SJ486, and Miss Belle MacKay at Lochranza, for the use of her five–seat Ford SJ501. These, with the maroon six–seat Overland SJ463 of S. Sillars at Shiskine, or SJ447, a goods/passenger convertible belonging to Malcolm MacKenzie at Machrie, would have been the most likely, since they were registered for hire or reward. Having thus arranged for his passengers to continue their tour, he would not have had far to look for a horse or two.

The Dodge was taken off that run after that, and one of the lighter vehicles was used until after 1929, when the building programme for stone bridges over burns which had been forded until then also included upgrading of some of the roads.

By 1930 there were several Currie taxis at Brodick Pier, in addition to a regular omnibus connection at least three times a day, in summer, to Shiskine and Blackwaterfoot. The omnibus fare was, by this time, three shillings (15p) single, and five shillings and six pence (27½p) return. No conductors were ever carried on Currie omnibuses.

By 1938 some lorries (which later passed to Lennox of Whiting Bay) were acquired, with several more from MacRae's with their cars and omnibuses. The fleet also had an Albion sun saloon 16–seater SJ688 new to Currie in 1932, and a Bedford WLB coach in that year. Winter times of omnibuses in 1936 were:

WEEKDAYS
Leave Shiskine 0600 arrive Brodick 0650†
Wait in Brodick, after departure of 0700 steamer
Leave Brodick 1115 arrive Blackwaterfoot 1200
Leave Shiskine 1500 arrive Brodick 1550†
Wait in Brodick 1900 arrive Blackwaterfoot 1950

†Light to Blackwaterfoot — officially at any rate — and start from there.

SUNDAYS
No service

All touring coaches and charabancs, as well as most of the cars, were laid up for the winter, and the immediate return from Brodick was not necessary at 0700 after June of that year; the Post Office introduced its own mail vans at that date, and handled its own mail carriage from Brodick to all parts of the island. The four vans, all of Morris manufacture, are shown later outside what was the post office then (and Pelligrini's shop now). John Currie died in 1940 and his widow sold out to Ribbecks in 1946.

It has not been possible to find a picture of John Currie, but the photograph on Plate 119 is of Col, the man who introduced the Postbus *and* the motor omnibus to Arran, and in addition laid down the tradition that "The man who carries the packman, carries the pack."

BRODICK TO BLACKWATERFOOT COMPETITORS

1884 advertisement

BANNATYNE, Blackwaterfoot. Sometime in the 1870s the
Carriage and Wagon Superintendent of the Caledonian Railway was
asked to consider the notion of fitting upholstered seats into the third
class carriages used on the Clyde Coast lines. His reply — "Coom oot,
ye want too much!" — may have been acceptable then, but 50 years on
it was quite clear that with three railway companies competing for the
passengers who wanted to travel to Arran and other places in the
Clyde that everything they wanted would have to be supplied. The
Glasgow & South Western Railway, the North British Railway and the
Caledonian Steam Packet Company, a subsidiary of the Caledonian
Railway, all ran passenger steamers to the eastern side of Arran.

   This conclusion was no less clear to Arran hoteliers, one of whom
was John Sillars Bannatyne, who provided a horse-drawn omnibus
service from Blackwaterfoot over the String Road to Brodick during
the 1920s and early 1930s.

A one-ton Ford dual-purpose chassis was obtained in about 1923, and this took the place of the horse-drawn vehicle on the service run. The driver was responsible for collecting the fares, an easy enough task on a 15–seat vehicle, and it appears that there were times in the summer when the omnibus had to make a double trip to cope with the number of passengers to and from Brodick. Since J. S. Bannatyne had no business with the mail, it is unlikely that he went in to Brodick for the first steamer arrival of the day. I have not been able to find any record of the times of the omnibus, although Mrs. E. McLeod told me recently that she remembers having to walk over Machrie Moor in time to get to the stone pillar box on the String road for 1030 in order to catch the Bannatyne omnibus.

The Ford omnibus was painted red, and according to the notes kindly supplied by Bob Grieves, J. S. Bannatyne also had the following tour cars — SJ304, a dark blue Ford registered in 1921; SJ449, a grey Ford registered in 1924; and SJ479, a green Buick registered in 1925. The first two listed were four–seaters, the Buick was a six–seater, and an anecdote told by its driver will be found in the chapter relating to the activities of the MacRae brothers, to whom J. S. Bannatyne sold out in 1935.

MACRAE, Blackwaterfoot. William and Duncan MacRae first appeared on the scene in 1935 when they took over the omnibus, garage and service of J. S. Bannatyne, together with the ex–McNeil FIAT, surplus to the requirement of Gordon Bros., Lamlash. Most of the people who remember them describe them as astute businessmen, so it is likely that they gave careful consideration to the passenger potential of the String road before deciding to continue the competition that J. S. Bannatyne had given to Currie's of Shiskine.

Certainly they were efficient — a large blackboard dominated one wall of their office, and on this Duncan's wife used to write the vehicle requirements as they arose. No entry was erased from the board until the vehicle marked down for the duty in question was rolling.

All of the vehicles were in the company colours of red and blue, although all of the MacRae vehicles were second-hand, the buses and coaches were painted before going on to the road for MacRae service. I have heard, but cannot obtain any confirmation, that the hire cars were also repainted red and blue as soon as they were obtained. There were about half a dozen cars in the fleet, and one of the drivers, Joe Hartley, told me that even in fine weather the canvas roofs had to be kept up as the radiators tended to boil over and spray back. At 36 h.p. the cars were more powerful than the omnibuses and coaches!

Competition with the Currie service was intense, although Mrs. Currie never forgot old Col's maxim that "The man who carries the packman carries the pack." The MacRae brothers soon found that attempts to load passengers into their own vehicles, and the passengers' luggage into a Currie vehicle were 'not on'. Tales have been handed down of acrimonious scenes at Brodick Pier, when drivers of the rival firms — and not just on the String road route — accosted potential passengers, and attempts to carry the bags to one vehicle would be hindered by the drivers of other omnibuses. This may surprise readers who are familiar with the provisions of the 1930 Road Traffic Act, but it *is* of the 1930s, *not* the 1920s that I am writing.

William and Duncan MacRae turned to goods haulage after a few years, and sold their omnibuses and coaches to their one-time rival, Currie's Motors, in 1938.

Brodick Pier, Spring 1980. Midland Red driver on holiday heard to comment that the Arran omnibus drivers do not know what mainland bus driving is like. Among the drivers present were Alistair McKenzie, ex-PMT, Alistair Nicholson, ex-Highland, Bill Harris, ex-Thames Valley. Later that day, after a trip round the island on the 10A Tour, same man was heard to remark that "A Midland Red driver wouldn't last five minutes here!"

RIBBECK, Brodick, Blackwaterfoot.
Brodick — Corrie — Sannox — Lochranza — Catacol
Brodick — Shiskine — Blackwaterfoot.

Adolph and Ernest Ribbeck came to Arran in the 1860s with, or just after, Princess Marie of Baden, who had married the 11th Duke of Hamilton. Although their presence in Arran appears to have been planned as a temporary one — they appear to have come only to paint the castle gates! — they did, in fact, stay here. Both of them married Arran girls and Adolph started a business which included what is nowadays that Aladdin's Cave of gifts, Alexanders of Brodick; and a photography business which has ensured that his name survives today on many photograph frames in the island.

Ernest became sub-postmaster at Brodick and took over the operation of the Corrie mail run as well. In 1879 he introduced a mail car on this route, which was running every day during the summer, and three times, at least, a week in winter. This was discontinued for a short time in 1887 or 1888, but was restored the following year. The reason for this is not known it was something to do with the 'mail' side of the facility. After 1888 the mail car was there to stay, and when Ernest's son, Kaspar, took over as operator of the mail coach (as it had by then become known) and as postman — although not as postmaster — the route was extended to Sannox.

Kaspar Ribbeck introduced the first bus tickets to Arran when, in 1899–1901, the service to Corrie and Sannox became so popular that a reservation had to be made, and a ticket for it obtained for any stated journey, and the sooner application was made for a 'place' in the coach, the more likely the chance of obtaining one.

The outbreak of the Great War led to a series of what could be described as absurd precautions and sanctions against Kaspar Ribbeck by the authorities responsible for the running of the Post Office. "Absurd" has always struck me as a word which includes a degree of fun, and since, despite glowing testimonials — all of which were unsolicited — from many prominent people, including a Member of Parliament, and despite public protest, Kaspar Ribbeck was more or less officially excluded from the Brodick Post Office, which was in a building he owned, and in spite of 50 years' residence in Arran, during which time the Ribbecks had the respect and affection of their neighbours, the German origins of the family was held against them by the policy of the government of the day — not the most tasteful tale in the history of British government policy. His daughter, born in Arran, was allowed to remain in the employ of the Post Office only if she moved to a less sensitive area (from a military point of view, that is. The Naval Base at Lamlash seems to have been the problem), and Kaspar was permitted to drive his own vehicle only on the Corrie mail route with mail in it if accompanied by a postman who was employed solely for that purpose.

At the end of the Great War, Kaspar Ribbeck devoted his attention to passenger transport, and severed his connection (which had, by then, been allowed again) with the Post Office.

A motor omnibus was obtained and it joined the rapidly-growing fleet of horse-drawn vehicles in 1919. Although Ribbeck is now one of the first names to come to the mind of anyone deciding to buy a motor car or have it serviced, in those days it was not so, and Kaspar had to go to Johnny Anderson at Pirnmill for a T–Ford which, like the one which was sold to Stewart in the same year, had solid tyres at one end. It was green, the standard Ribbeck colour for the next twenty years, and was used as an omnibus on the Brodick to Corrie (and later to Sannox) route. Tickets for seats were no longer required in advance, and although it was sometimes necessary to duplicate the motor omnibus with a horse-drawn vehicle, the passengers, to whom part-printed, part-handwritten tickets were issued by this time, were never left behind.

The first motor charabanc, acquired for tours, had what were described as 'Giant Pneumatic Tyres', known locally as 'balloon tyres'. This was a great success — it was an Albion, rather more advanced that Col Currie's first machine, of course, and during its first

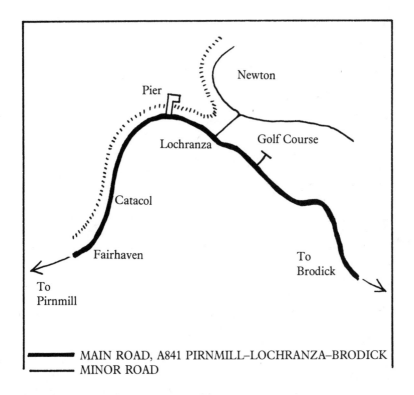

MAIN ROAD, A841 PIRNMILL–LOCHRANZA–BRODICK
MINOR ROAD

When the steamer ran from Glasgow to Campbeltown Lochranza was a busy place. Terminal points were:

RIBBECK & KERR-NEWTON, from Brodick to Catacol, turning at 'Fairhaven' and back to the pier, from where journeys to Brodick were commenced.
ANDERSON & McMILLAN (up to 1929) from Pirnmill to the Lochranza Pier only.
WEIR & ROBERTSON through the village to the Golf Course, then back to the pier, from where south-bound journeys commenced.
BANNATYNE MOTORS, to the pier only, then return to the south.

touring season in 1921 it was given the name *The Viking*. A second Albion was ordered in the hope that it would be in time for the end of the 1921 season, but, in fact, it was 1922 before it arrived. To this second machine the name *The Valkyrie* was given. By the end of that season the fame and popularity of the two Albion charas had got back to Albion Motors at Scotstoun, Glasgow, and the story goes that Albion sought Kaspar Ribbeck's permission to use the names *Valkyrie* and *Viking* for types of chassis they were thinking of producing in the near future.

A large card advertisement was produced, giving the times of omnibuses to Corrie and Sannox on one side, with a photograph of *The Viking* and a description of the various tours to be had on the obverse. One of these advertisements, together with some other incredibly rare tickets, which has survived in almost mint condition during the intervening sixty years, was very generously given to me by several members of the Ribbeck family not so long ago, and they are, without a doubt, the most impressive bits of transport company literature I have ever seen from any age (I exclude the front cover of the 1963 timetable of the Devon General Omnibus & Touring Co. Ltd. from this comparison, only on the grounds that, unlike Ribbeck's, it is in colour!).

The tours offered were:

The Island Tour which left Brodick at 11 a.m. on Mondays, Wednesdays and Fridays. It passed through Corrie, Sannox and Lochranza, turning off the coast road at Machrie, from where it went over the moor, then turned right on to the String Road, which it followed to Shedog, Shiskine, where a stop was made for lunch. After lunch it went on to Blackwaterfoot and around the south of the island, via Low Kildonan, arriving back in Brodick at about 4 p.m. The fare, which did not include lunch, was ten shillings (50p).

The Macrihanish Tour — To the Shores of the Atlantic was scheduled to depart from Brodick on Tuesdays, Thursdays and Saturdays at 10 a.m., and run non-stop to Lochranza, where the passengers joined the turbine steamer *King Edward* (the first turbine-powered passenger steamer in the world, put into service twenty years previously by a syndicate which included The Hon. Charles Parsons, James Denny and Captain John Williamson). On arrival at Campbeltown passengers

1884 Advertisement

were transferred to a train of the Campbeltown & Macrihanish Light Railway, or — depending on the day — a charabanc of the West Coast Motors, for the final leg of the journey to the Atlantic shore. The tour was scheduled to arrived back at Lochranza by 4 p.m., and at Brodick by 5.30 p.m. The fare was six shillings (30p) for the coach, and 2/6d (12½p) for the steamer, a worthwhile reduction from the standard steamer return fare. It is even more interesting to see that ten shillings was charged for a journey taking more than 70 miles of road (*Island Tour*), and yet that more than half of that price was charged for less than half of that distance by road on the Macrihanish tour. Further, passengers for the Macrihanish tour were taken to Lochranza for one shilling (5p) more than the passengers to the same place in the evening when the *Evening Cruise to Lochranza* left Brodick at 7.30 p.m. on Saturdays, which allowed one hour at Lochranza before setting off back for an arrival in Brodick by 10 p.m. *The Viking* was allowed 1½ hours to get to Lochranza on the Macrihanish tour, yet the evening cruise, which did not go beyond that village, was allowed only half the time to get there.

Viking and *Valkyrie* were both used on these tours as and when demand for seats was high enough. At other times they took it turn and turn about.

The omnibus route Brodick—Corrie—Sannox, ran empty from Brodick each day to pick up incoming passengers from Sannox at 6.15 a.m., and picked up at Corrie at 6.30, arriving back in Brodick at 7 a.m. A note in the timetable states that this departure was made only "if required". Services for the rest of the day, and each day in the summer, were:

Leave:

Brodick 1100	Sannox 1415
Corrie 1130	Corrie 1430
Sannox 1140	Brodick 1500

Presumably the driver lived at Sannox, and there was a lay-over there between 1140 and 1415. It is not likely that Kaspar Ribbeck would have countenanced a machine running back to Brodick and out to Corrie again at these times without advertising it on the timetable. The run back from Sannox must have been busy, in view of

the fact that there was an extra five minutes allowed on the return
journey between there and Sannox. The omnibus left Brodick again at
3:45 p.m. and got to Sannox at 4.25. Every day, except Saturdays, it
left Sannox again at 5.20 p.m., and arrived back in Brodick at 6 p.m.
From there it went straight back to Sannox, arriving at 6.50 p.m., and
returned in service at once to Brodick, with 15 minutes allowed
between Sannox and Corrie. In later years extra omnibuses were put
on to carry the workers to and from the barytes mine at Sannox. The
single fare was two shillings (10p).

The service was extended to Lochranza in 1926 and to Catacol in
1930, after which date competition from, then co-operation with, F. K.
Newton (in the shape of North Arran Motors) was the order of the day.
An omnibus of either participant on a turn and turn about basis was
despatched from Brodick at 5 a.m., to run 'light' to Catacol in time to
leave there and uplift all passengers on the way in to the steamer which
left Brodick at 7 a.m. The fare was 2/6d (12½p) at first, but was raised
to 3/6d (17p) within a year of the Catacol extension.

A regular tour of the 1920s and 1930s was an outing on which most
of Ribbeck's (and other services) drivers and their families went
regularly.

At its zenith the Ribbeck fleet was a sizeable one, including as it did
the vehicles taken over with the Brodick to Blackwaterfoot route of
Currie's (which was not part of the North Arran Motors pooling
arrangement with Finlay Kerr-Newton).

After 1946, all Ribbeck omnibuses and coaches were repainted blue
and cream, and most of them had a swallow painted on the side, a motif
which was also to be found on the blazer badges issued to the drivers.

In 1946 the North Arran omnibus service which had been drastically
reduced during the Second German War was restored to its pre-war
frequency of a departure each way every half hour to Lochranza, and
every hour to and from Catacol. The Currie's omnibus and coach fleet,
as already mentioned, was taken over in that year, and tours were once
again put in hand, including an arrangement for the Arran end of a
mystery tour promoted by an English operator in which a seven-
day trip, promising a journey starting in the English coaches,
transferring on to a ship, then on to another set of coaches, at a

destination withheld from the passengers, was advertised in and around a Lancashire coastal resort.

The North Arran Motors arrangement came to an end in 1952, when Finlay Kerr-Newton retired; from then on, Ribbecks were the sole operators of omnibuses between Brodick and Catacol. In addition, the String Road service to Shiskine and Blackwaterfoot was handed over to the newly-formed Bannatyne Motors.

Ribbeck's Motors still sell, service, maintain and repair cars and other motor vehicles at their Brodick garage, but the omnibuses and coaches were sold to Arran Transport in 1966.

KERR-NEWTON, Brodick
Brodick — Corrie — Sannox — Lochranza — Catacol

Finlay Kerr-Newton was one of the few busmen in Arran who did not drift into the passenger transport industry 'with the tide'. By 1930, the year he purchased the Pier Garage in Brodick with its vehicles from Neil McBride, the days of piracy were over. Omnibus operation had been put on to a regular footing — or at least they were running on a regulated basis. For this reason, or maybe in spite of it, Finlay Kerr-Newton saw great possibilities in Arran's passenger transport industry. It may be that he envisaged even greater potential for tourism than had been foreseen by others already 'on the road'. Certainly, while other operators put omnibuses *and* coaches into service, the vehicles of Finlay Kerr-Newton were always of a type which could be used for tours and private hire (the kind of machine which today would be called a dual-purpose vehicle, having an omnibus body, but with coach-type seats).

The fleet with which he had started included a FIAT, which had been used by McBride, to establish a route between the piers at Lochranza and Brodick. This was disposed of and a green and cream Chevrolet sun saloon SJ649 took its place. The FIAT (as Fiat vehicles were known in those days) went 'abroad' and SJ447, the Overland goods interchangeable which had come from Malcolm MacKenzie at Machrie in 1928, was sold to Latona, a Brodick haulage contractor. There were, initially, two north Arran tours operated in the summers 1931–1934, with the Brodick–Lochranza omnibus running in competition with the Ribbeck service. Two Commer *Avenger* saloon coaches were ordered, and arrived in time to take over the summer tours from the 1935 season. They were green and yellow, the same as the Chevrolet, and had roll-top roofs which may have given them a slight edge at that time over the fixed roof coaches of the rival Ribbeck. It was in 1935 that the omnibus route was extended to Catacol, giving an overlap of two miles between Catacol and Lochranza, with the Robertson and the Weir services from Blackwaterfoot and Machrie, which turned at Lochranza Golf Club, and not at the pier.

The fare in the early 1930s was one shilling (5p) from Brodick to Corrie and 3/6d (17½p) to Lochranza. Drivers and conductors wore a green linen jacket, with a slightly darker green collar, and the legend *Newton's Brodick* in the form of a chromed brooch.

In 1936, Newton's Motors won a contract to supply coaches for use on tours in connection with steamers arriving at Lochranza Pier. Omnibuses already connected, of course, but this was a 'package' booked through the steamer company. At the same time, Finlay Kerr-Newton arranged with the steamer company and with the Campbeltown and Macrihanish Light Railway Company for a tour originating in Brodick, Corrie, Sannox and Catacol on a Newton's coach, transferring to a steamer at Lochranza, and from the steamer to the Light Railway at Campbeltown for a return trip across the Kintyre peninsula. This was basically a day trip to Campbeltown, with an extra shilling (5p) being added to the cost of the ticket of anyone who wanted to take a hurl on the train. He must have done some tough negotiating with the C. & M.L.R because the return fare for a Campbeltown to Macrihanish trip booked at the offices of the railway cost more than that.

One of the regular drivers in the 1930s was Archie Currie of Brodick who often drove the north Arran or all-Arran tour which left Brodick at around 1000 each day. On one such day he had in his party a woman of the type known and detested by coach drivers the world over. No sooner had Archie pointed out the Castle than this particular woman was heard to interrupt Archie with a short history of it. When Archie drew breath from pointing out the Doctor's Bath at Corrie, and was just about to give details, they came from the back of the coach loud and clear. The same happened when he drew up at the top of the hill on the Sannox–Lochranza road to point out the Sleeping Warrior. The lady had it all off pat, and could not restrain herself from telling all of the others in the coach. On the way down into Lochranza, a party of tinkers was encountered, pushing their prams along the road.

"I suppose that they are local people", said the lady.

A gleam came into Archie's eyes, and without taking his gaze from the road ahead, he replied in a very loud, but courteous voice:

"No, Madam, they are visitors" he paused to change gear, then added "just like you are.".

Archie told me that he had no more interruptions for the rest of the tour.

In the early 1940s things were difficult for omnibus operators. I've said as much in previous chapters and probably will say so again before the end of this book, but it is forty years since the Second German War, and many people born since then may not realise that all of Britain's oil and petrol, as well as rubber for tyres, had to be shipped in from abroad, and there was no finer target for an unterzeeboot than a big tanker. I once heard it said that only 60% of tankers reached Britain, and in any case that all of them which started out totalled less than in peacetime. So, with petrol, oil and tyres — to name but three essential commodities — being despatched at a reduced rate, and with 40% of these shipments not arriving, it is easy to understand that coach tours and omnibus services were reduced. Add to this the fact that most able-bodied men either volunteered or were conscripted into the forces (burning of draft-cards — fortunately — had not been thought of) the omnibus companies were short of everything. Short of drivers, mechanics, spares, tyres and fuel though they were, Arran's omnibus services — in skeleton form at any rate — were regarded as being 'essential rural services', and were not withdrawn, or forced to withdraw, like the Green Line serving London had been. To cope with a fairly high demand for omnibus services on top of a reduced capability, Finlay Kerr-Newton came to a 'pooling' arrangement with his rival Ribbeck. The Brodick—Corrie—Sannox—Lochranza—Catacol service became 'North Arran Motors'. This was a similar set-up to that arranged between Lennox's and Gordon Bros., and in this case, the omnibuses of the two participants ran in their separate colours, with the legal lettering reading *F. K. NEWTON* or *E. K. RIBBECK* as the case may be, and the fleet name *NORTH ARRAN MOTORS* on the sides of the omnibuses. Tickets were interchangeable on the north Arran route, and some journeys which had previously run through to Catacol were terminated at Lochranza Pier.

The pooling arrangement did not embrace the Brodick—String Road—Shiskine—Blackwaterfoot omnibus route which had passed to Ribbeck in 1946; Ribbeck's Motors and only Ribbeck's Motors operated that route when it was taken over with the Currie company. At the same time, competition for private hire and tours, when these became possible again after the war, was just as intense as previously.

Finlay Kerr-Newton used to give his personal attention to the loading of Lochranza-bound omnibuses at Brodick Pier, and so arranged it that Lochranza passengers boarded first, so that any passengers alighting at Corrie and Sannox did not have to squeeze past them, and their luggage and 'messages' in the gangway. In the late 1940s and the first two years of the 1950s, there was an omnibus from Brodick to Lochranza and back every half hour, and from Brodick to Catacol every hour during the summer months.

In 1952, Newton's Motors had eight vehicles, three of them were omnibuses in the North Arran Motors pool the other five were coaches. These, several taxis and the Pier Garage at Brodick, were sold to Lennox, and the north Arran route became Ribbeck's exclusively in that year when Finlay Kerr-Newton bowed out of the omnibus scene into retirement.

An old lady in Whiting Bay had difficulty in climbing the front steps of a bus. The driver made a joke of it by saying that he would lower the step for her. So saying, he twirled the handle that changes the destination screen, for a dozen or so turns. "It should be low enough now," he said. "Give it a try." "Just right." said the old lady and skipped up the steps like a two-year-old.

HAMILTON, High Kildonan
Lagg Hotel—Kilmory—High Kildonan—Dippen
—Largiebeg—Whiting Bay Pier

Like Davidson of Brodick, John Hamilton seems to have made a regular trip to the pier (in this case at Whiting Bay) just for passengers and goods, since he had no mail contract. It is likely that this was on a once-a-week basis, when he first began his service in 1889. Prior to this date he had made regular trips from Drumla, High Kildonan, with produce from his farm. These would have been eastward to the pier at Whiting Bay and, at other times, westward to the Lagg Hotel, from where he received orders for farm produce. The idea of a passenger cart appears to have originated from the Lagg Hotel, and in all probability the photograph taken in 1889 (Plate 13) was to mark the start of what was certainly envisaged only as a hotel omnibus, and although passengers along the way were carried, the departures from, and arrivals at, the Lagg Hotel would have been for the benefit and to the requirement of the hotel guests.

This state of affairs continued until 1895, when John Hamilton died and his brother, Sandy Hamilton, took over the direction of the business. Sandy was very keen to increase the transport side of his farming and haulage activities, and within a very short time had arranged to export some of his services. This was a time, you will recollect, when Glasgow-based carriage hirers were still obtaining business by sending coaches with liveried drivers to Arran. Sandy not only held his own against them but did fairly well out of sending his own conveyances to the mainland for such functions as the Ayr Show. By 1905, at the age of 40 — John had been 39 when he died — Sandy Hamilton had a twice-weekly omnibus service running between Lagg and Whiting Bay, over and above the requirement for the hotel, and in

1884 advertisement   xvii

LAGG HOTEL,

KILMORY,

ARRAN,

Nine Miles from Whiting Bay, and about the same
distance from Lamlash,

**Is pleasantly situated, and a favourite
resort for Excursionists.**

Right of Fishing reserved for Hotel Visitors.

Every attention given to Tourists.

CHARGES MODERATE.

CONVEYANCES TO BE HAD ON HIRE.

JAMES DEWAR,

PROPRIETOR.

addition had brought his haulage side (mainly of his own, and other farmers' produce) to its peak.

The motor omnibus fleet came into being just after the Great War when the Commer charabanc SJ146 was purchased from the Jamieson sisters at Kildonan. This was soon followed by a one-ton Ford dual-purpose, SJ299, which was used by the farm, for passengers, for the hotel and for the omnibus service, leaving the Commer, and an Albion (1924, ex-Lennox) for tours. In connection with the tours, it is perhaps worth recording here that one of the first Round Arran tours was operated by John Hamilton, using a horse-drawn charabanc, for the guests of the Lagg Hotel. On one of the first of these tours, the Shannochie Postmistress, who had been invited to join the tour, sent a telegram from the overnight stopping place at Lochranza: "Have arrived safely". The second overnight stop was at Whiting Bay. It is difficult to believe today, when an A.T.T. coach can drive right around the island in less than six hours, including stops.

In 1924 a Dodge charabanc SJ485 had joined the fleet new and a grey 14–seat Ford charabanc SJ343 is also said to have been purchased at the same time, second-hand presumably since the registration number is earlier than 1924. No trace of the original owner has come to hand. At the end of the summer of 1926, Sandy Hamilton discontinued his omnibus and tour business. This appears to have been a sudden decision in view of his purchases the previous year. Further, his expressed intention to re-start his activities the following year would support this. In the event, he did not re-start, his vehicles had all been sold, and Donald Stewart had been asked to alter his own omnibus services to fill the gap.

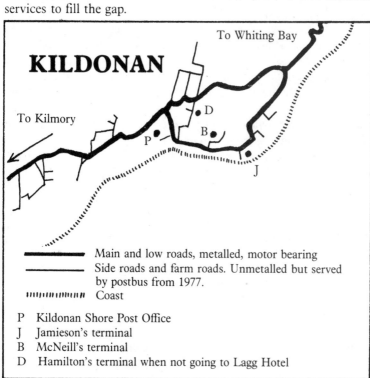

KILDONAN

To Whiting Bay

To Kilmory

P
D
B
J

————— Main and low roads, metalled, motor bearing
————— Side roads and farm roads. Unmetalled but served
         by postbus from 1977.
⅏⅏⅏⅏⅏⅏ Coast

P   Kildonan Shore Post Office
J   Jamieson's terminal
B   McNeill's terminal
D   Hamilton's terminal when not going to Lagg Hotel

JAMIESON, Low Kildonan
Kildonan Hotel – Dippen – Whiting Bay Pier

There are many cases in the British Isles of hotels providing some form of transport for their guests and staff who wish to travel between the hotel and the nearest railway station. Sometimes a local carrier or coachman was retained for the job, and sometimes the hotel provided a hotel omnibus and driver of its own. There were even cases of a railway company (the London & South Western coming at once to mind) providing a regular service so regular indeed, that the name of the hotel and the name of the railway station from which it ran were painted on the side of the vehicle. Further, the Cruden Bay Hotel had a tramway, complete with electric tram service, linking it with the Great North of Scotland Railway (later to form part of the L.N.E.).

In all cases, the hotel omnibus, hotel cart, hotel tram — whatever form of vehicle used — was solely for the use of hotel guests and staff. I know of no instance, (although I'd like to hear of one) where the hotel conveyance was available to passengers along the way. Of course, this may no longer be the case in these days following that incredibly foolish piece of legislation, the Transport Act of October 1980, but insofar as the period covered by this book is concerned, I know of only one hotel omnibus which was available to intending passengers along the way on a regular time and pre-arranged fare basis.

The case in question is that of the Jamieson brothers who ran the Kildonan Hotel and provided a conveyance to and from the Pier at Whiting Bay. The service seems to have started in 1880, with a horse-drawn brake, and after 1900 the brake, or a later addition to the fleet, made a daily run to and from Kildonan, even when not required to do so by guests or staff.

xvi   1884 advertisement

KILDONAN HOTEL,
ARRAN.

DELIGHTFULLY situated, and is in the immediate vicinity of the old Castle of Kildonan. Tourists may rely on receiving every attention.

The locality is famed for Salt and Fresh Water Fishing, and the Beach is unsurpassed for Bathing.

BOATS CAN BE HAD ON HIRE.

CONVEYANCE
To and from Whiting Bay on arrival and departure of Steamers.

JAMES JAMIESON,
Proprietor.

In 1914 a grey Albion motor charabanc was purchased, the second motor omnibus to arrive in Arran. This took over the omnibus route, leaving the horse-drawn vehicles free to take hotel guests on picnic trips, bathing parties and the like. Both horse-drawn vehicles, and the Albion, were also used for tours from time to time, and when I asked the only surviving driver if these tours were for hotel guests or local people, he replied "Yes"!

A Commer charabanc, SJ146, was registered to J. J. Jamieson in 1914, thus bringing the fleet up to four vehicles, two horse-drawn and two motor-driven. The petrol shortage during the Great War necessitated greater use of the horse-drawn vehicles, one of which had "a wee wheel at the back for a brake", but the licensing of a Ford model-T, SJ162 in 1916 would indicate that the shortage was overcome – or that a motor vehicle was essential, and that the Ford was chosen for economy.

The Jamieson brothers died within a short time of each other in 1917, and their two sisters sold the vehicles to Hamilton, who, with McNeill, filled the gap left in the road, a year later.

In general many rural areas tend to have two categories of resident; those who are born in the area are known to themselves and others as "natives" and those who moved in from elsewhere are called "incomers". One of the drivers on a south Arran omnibus in the early 1930s was noted for the discrimination he showed towards "incomers". Nothing nasty, you understand, but as far as he was concerned "incomers" were a different species. A south Arran girl married a man from the mainland and, after the honeymoon, the couple returned to Arran to live. They got off the steamer at Whiting Bay and boarded the south Arran omnibus. The man asked for "Two to Lagg' and was told by the driver that it would be: "1/6d for you, and 1/3d for your wife."

McNEILL, Kildonan
Kildonan (Breadalbane Hotel) – Low Road – Dippen –Whiting Bay Pier

One of the best-remembered passenger carriers in south Arran was William McNeill, who lived in Kildonan. He had the contract to carry mails between Kildonan and Whiting Bay and, in addition, had the Breadalbane Hotel at Kildonan, so he had interests in transport as well. At the turn of the century these interests were reflected in a fleet of 'singles' and 'doubles', that is to say wagonnettes and carts drawn by one or two horses respectively; and by 1905 he had a three-horse charabanc which he used for hires, and only for hires at that time, to and from the steamer at Whiting Bay, and for tours.

He does not seem to have considered utilising his trips between Kildonan and Whiting Bay for carrying passengers on an omnibus basis until 1910. Possibly he considered that there were sufficient omnibuses already on the road, but in the summer of 1910 he started to use the three-horse charabanc for this purpose, charging three shillings (15p) return. The journey took one hour, "although we could do it in much less time than that" as one of his ex-drivers once told me. There were no covers at all on the three-horse charabanc, and the first motor omnibus, when it came to Kildonan, had little more than a token roof — it would seem that one had to be one of Britain's hardy sons (or daughters) to ride in a McNeill vehicle in those days.

The first motor omnibus SJ357, a blue 14–seat FIAT charabanc, arrived in 1922, followed by a second, identical machine, SJ405 in 1923, although it is not possible to establish if this came second-hand from McBride, Brodick, or was passed on to him, but in any case, by 1924 there were two FIAT charabancs (and McBride still had one), with SJ442 a 14–seat blue Ford added in the summer of that year,

together with two remarkable machines – 16-seat Rolls-Royce charabancs, of which I'll have more to say in a later chapter.

After 1925, tours were advertised on a daily basis, and were operated
up to Lamlash and back over the Ross Road, and occasionally one
went up as far as Lochranza. The omnibus service to Whiting Bay was
operated on a regular and frequent basis during sumer months, but in
the winter, when the tours were withdrawn, the service to Whiting Bay
was reduced to a bare minimum, and does not, in any case, seem to
have run every day. During winter months a full-time mechanic gave a
complete overhaul to each of the vehicles. One of the FIAT machines
was serviced first, and this then took over the winter service for the
first three months, while all of the other vehicles received attention. At
the end of the first three months of winter operation the first FIAT was
taken off the road and overhauled again, while one of the other FIAT
vehicles took its place on the road. The two Rolls-Royce charabancs
were laid up immediately after overhaul for the winter.

A Halley saloon coach was purchased in 1933. It had a 15–seat front-
entrance body, and was the only closed-top vehicle in the fleet. It
operated most the scheduled omnibus departures, leaving the charabancs free to provide tours, for which there was great demand in the
1933, 1934 and 1935 seasons, after which William McNeill sold his
omnibuses and coaches, together with the goodwill, to Gordon Bros.,
Lamlash, and thereby hangs a tale.

For some long-forgotten — and maybe best-forgotten — reason,
William McNeill and A. C. Lennox, an omnibus operator at Whiting
Bay, did not get on. I do not want to dwell on old feuds, and indeed I've
come across many during the research for this book which I see no
point in airing, but this one is essential to the anecdote concerning the
handover. Certainly both William McNeill and A. C. Lennox were
well thought of by their contemporaries, both were well-respected in
the community, as indeed are their descendants, and I can only assume
that it was a minor misunderstanding. Whatever the reason, Pa
Lennox made several offers to William McNeill during the period 1932
to 1935. Pa was forced to share his road with Gordon Bros., as we shall
see in a later chapter, and his offer to buy up McNeill, if accepted,
would, he felt, give him an edge over his arch-rivals, the Gordon
brothers. Offers for the business were made to McNeill at regular

intervals, and Pa was given an assurance that they would be considered. However, when, in 1935, McNeill decided to sell out, he approached Gordons with a proposition.

Gordon Bros Motors were offered the omnibus route, the tours, the goodwill, and the vehicles at a very reasonable price. The conditions were that the men employed at Kildonan were retained, that Gordons would have to find other premises, since McNeill's premises could not be included in the deal. The main condition, however, was that not a word was said to Lennox, and that the ex-McNeill vehicles were repainted behind locked doors, overnight, into the Gordon livery, and that McNeill himself would drive the first scheduled departure from Kildonan to Whiting Bay on the first day under new management.

And so it happened. The Kildonan drivers were kept on, and a local hall obtained and converted to a garage. All of the vehicles were repainted into the light blue, red, and dark blue of Gordon's late one night behind the closed doors of the 'new' garage, except for one FIAT, which went to MacRae's of Blackwaterfoot. Thus the McNeill business passed to Gordon's in 1935.

As for Pa Lennox, the first he knew of it was on the first day of the new regime, when a loud prolonged blast of a motor horn took him to the door of his office in Whiting Bay just in time to see one of the Rolls-Royce machines, on which he had set his heart, in the colours of his rival, being driven by William McNeill, who acknowledged his presence with a time-honoured gesture.

ROLLS-ROYCE —
A FIVE YEAR SEARCH

This following will be a digression from the story traced in this book and, even now, I am not sure if it is a good idea to include it as readers may not be interested in the trials and tribulations of the researcher. However, those of you not inclined to follow me through a catalogue of searching, drawing blank, giving up, then getting there, are at liberty to turn the pages until a new heading is reached, since it will be at that point that I'll return to the theme of this book.

I first heard the name Rolls-Royce mentioned in the context of omnibuses while talking to Alan and Donald McNeill in the summer of 1976. They gave me as much information as they could remember about the omnibuses and coaches their father ran, as well as the names of some of the ex-drivers who might be able to add to what they had told me. Not surprisingly, they were unable to give me a day-to-day account of what happened forty years ago, particularly since they were quite young then, and not particularly interested in the nuts and bolts of their father's business.

The driver to whom I was introduced by Alan and Donald, and people to whom I was sent on by them, all spoke of the "Rolls-Royces". Some said that there were two, some said that there were three, and the colours were described as white, yellow and even ivory. Some people even spoke of a black-and-white check band around them, and a belted device on the side. Since, with the best will in the world, elderly people can at times have blurred memories of forty years before, since gossip and assumption, legend and fact, often become one in the clearest and youngest of minds, and since there were no photographs available of the Rolls-Royce machines, I tended to the view that these were, in fact, slightly less noble chassis on which Pullman-type bodies of an advanced and luxurious type had been fitted, and that the *nickname* Rolls-Royce had survived in a distorted form.

This was in 1976 and I glossed over the existence of these vehicles (which in any case I doubted) with a sentence in the McNeill chapter to the effect that two other motor charabancs, said to have been Rolls-Royce based, were added to the fleet. By this time I was living in Lamlash, opposite Ernest Gordon, one of the two brothers who ran Gordon's Motors, which took over from McNeill's in 1935. I was privileged to become a close friend of Ernest before he died and he was most insistent that they were Rolls-Royce machines, complete with that rather dreary Greek temple radiator. I was still not convinced, but I decided to keep an open mind on the subject, despite the fact that one of the chaps at Rolls-Royce Derby had stated quite positively that there had never been any such thing as a Rolls-Royce bus — after which he complained, no doubt, to the GPO that he had received an obscene telephone call!

Early in 1977, partly thanks to efforts made by Ernest Gordon and partly, I am sure, due to efforts made by Alan and Donald McNeill, I received a photograph of one of the Rolls-Royce machines, the one with the driver standing next to it in Whiting Bay. This established that there had, after all, been at least one of them, so I was prepared now to accept "two or three". All I needed to know was if there were two *or* three. I sent a copy of the photograph to Rolls-Royce ('no answer' was the stern reply!) and took my copy of the photograph to Ernest Gordon, who remembered that there had been only two. The first had been cut down in 1939–1940 for use as an agricultural plough tractor, and the other had been dismantled at about the same time and had its engine and transmission fitted into the shell of a Bedford saloon coach, thus turning the whole thing into a sawmill!

Icabod.

By this time I had established to my own satisfaction that there had been two of them, and I had further established what became of them.

During 1978, in the course of one of my many conversations with another elderly neighbour, Johnny Miller, I learned that these machines must have come from Rankin Brothers of Glasgow. Ernest had been unable to tell me where they had come from since his late brother had dealt with the matter, but Johnny Miller told me that they had been kept at Partick and operated until about 1924 by Rankins. I found this rather interesting since a 1923 Rankin Brothers advertisement was in my possession. So I reckoned that I had finally traced the entire story of these two vehicles, and assumed that they were ex-Great War armoured car chassis purchased by and bodied for Rankin Brothers, and was content to leave it at that.

In 1979 I found a handbook for a 1920 vintage Rolls-Royce motor car. It had been left in the cafeteria of Glasgow Central station. I traced this to Dr. John Corcoran of the University of Strathclyde and was able to return it to him. While doing so I mentioned the Arran Rolls-Royces of which he had never heard, but he put me in touch with John Fasal in London, whose history of the Rolls-Royce company had taken him to most of the countries in the world over the past 14 years. While most interested, he, too, knew nothing about them at all, and there the whole matter rested.

In 1980 Ken Wolverton, Arran's community artist, told me that there was a Rolls-Royce open-top single-deck bus in storage in Edinburgh and, for the next year, I wondered how two vehicles could be completely destroyed, when one apparently survived.

Finally, in mid-1981, Bob Grieves came over from Renfrew and introduced himself to me. He produced photographs of the outside of Rankins' offices, beside which were parked *more* than three Rolls-Royce charabancs, and told me that two came to Arran and the others disposed of elsewhere. The charabanc bodies were built by Cadogan of Perth. The two that came to Arran remained in Rankin colours of yellow until taken over by Gordon Brothers, but, during the period 1924–1930, the belted devices, the black-and-white checked bands and the fleet numbers — 75 and 77 — applied by Rankins, were removed by McNeill. On the subject of numbers, the registration number shown in the photograph on Plate 29 is a London issue, and if anyone can throw any light on that —

Following an accident between an Arran omnibus and a Ford saloon car, the omnibus driver entered the details of the car on his accident report form as a "Ford Concertina".

CURRIE, Kilmory
Lagg Hotel — Kilmory — Shannochie — Lavencorrach — High Kildonan — Dippen — Largiebeg — Whiting Bay

One of the busiest of all the mail carriers in Arran must surely have been Willie Currie. Whereas Col (a relative) and Donald Stewart (a neighbour) ran through sparsely-populated areas, Willie was stopping and starting as often as a present-day city omnibus. When Willie first started carrying the mail in 1889 he had a pony and trap, and a 'competitor' for passengers, although in fact the mail was Willie's main consideration. He would carry passengers in to Whiting Bay Pier early in the morning when he was going anyway to pick up the mail, and on the way back he stopped at many houses along the road to deliver mail, and while both Col Currie and Donald Stewart had a distance of at least seven miles in which there were no stops at all, Willie's route was reckoned in 'stops to the mile' rather than 'miles to the stop'.

In 1924 he decided to try a motor vehicle, and obtained SJ424, a light blue Ford wagonnette. He did not keep it for long. There are several reasons given for this, the main one being that with so many stops and starts he did not find it an economic proposition. He carried more passengers in the winter than the summer; when Hamilton did not run to and from Whiting Bay so often, Willie still had to go every day since a Royal Mail contract is not a thing to be discharged on a casual basis, and Willie was anything but casual in his duties for, and responsibilities to, the Post Office.

He offered the motor wagonette to John MacKenzie at King's Cross, but after due consideration John declined the offer and the machine was returned to the dealer, Anderson of Pirnmill.

In 1929 Willie was asked to include parts of Dippen and Low Kildonan in his 'walk' (which I understand to be the postman's term for his round or route). The parts of Dippen in question had, until then, been served by a 'runner' who took on the mail Willie dropped in bulk at Dippen Post Office, now closed. Willie, who was in any case nearing retirement age, declined to accept the extra mileage, and retired early.

Colin Currie of Shiskine may have been the first postman in the island to use a motor omnibus but Willie was the last to use a horse.

STEWART, Corriecravie, Whiting Bay
Corriecravie—Sliddery—Ross road—Lamlash
Blackwaterfoot—Corriecravie—Sliddery—
Lagg—Kildonan—Whiting Bay—
Lamlash—Brodick

There can be no dispute that the eight miles over the Ross road from Lamlash to the west coast are the most desolate and sparsely populated miles in Arran. Even today, especially during the winter, it is possible to travel its length without seeing a living soul. There are few houses on it, and none at all from Milepost 8 to Glen Scorrodale, where there is a farm, and from there to Glen Ree, where the houses start to appear again. As a means of communication it is of use only to people who want to go by car from Lamlash or Whiting Bay to Kilmory or Sliddery. Indeed, from Lamlash, it is as quick to go round the south to anywhere east of Kilmory Creamery.

Donald Stewart was using it in 1878 on a regular basis to take passengers in his purpose-built wagonette to Lamlash. So regular was the passenger service that the Post Office asked him to take the mails in and after 1879. Unlike Colin Currie who had utilised an existing mail run, or Kaspar Ribbeck, who had attempted both at the same time, Donald Stewart put his wagonette on to the road solely for passengers and tourists, and it was not until 1890 that Donald got an increased horse allowance, and there appears to have been a catch in it (see Currie, Shiskine, para.2), since he was more or less obliged to undertake two daily trips in the summer and a trip every day in the winter to cope with the increased demands on the mail. These were in part caused by the tourists who were coming to the island in ever-increasing numbers, so it may well have been a vicious circle so far as Donald Stewart was concerned.

In 1909 a brake was put on to the Ross road mail run, leaving the wagonette and a gig free for tours and private hire work, some of which would have come from the Lagg Hotel and from the larger houses at

Blackwaterfoot. The brake was a 10 seater, and ran twice a day during the summer months of 1909 to the start of the Great War, with the original wagonette, or the gig, used in the winter. (The gig was invariably on the road for the first two weeks of the winter — Jenny Stewart drove it while her father took a holiday). By 1914 there were two brakes, two gigs and a new wagonette.

The motor omnibus does not seem to have impressed Donald Stewart at first, or perhaps he was a bit late off the mark in ordering one before the Great War broke out. At any rate it was 1919 before he put one on to the road, a Ford model T brand new War Department specification, but diverted to Anderson, the Pirnmill dealer, when the war ended, before the batch it was in could be sent to the army and put to a rather more bellicose use than the one Donald Stewart had in mind. The body, a seven–seater with three-a-side and one next to the driver, was built by Cowieson of St. Rollox, Glasgow.

A year later the Ford one–ton dual purpose chassis was made available, and Donald Stewart obtained one. It had solid tyres on the rear axle, and pneumatic tyres on the front axle. It also came via Pirnmill and Cowieson's, with a 12–seat body, five each side and two up with the driver. Within a fortnight of its arrival the solid tyres had been removed and pneumatics fitted to the rear. Another one–ton Ford dual purpose chassis came in 1922. This time Donald Stewart built a body for it himself.

So far as I'm aware there were only two proper coachbuilders in Arran. One was a family firm, MacKenzies of Shiskine, who built wagonettes and vans — all horse-drawn — and since the home-made body remained on the one–ton chassis and gave satisfactory service for more than a decade, we can count Donald Stewart as the other 'proper coachbuilder'.

The 1922 Stewart-built vehicle had a detachable roof and removable seats, and was used at times as a lorry as well as a coach. It brought the Stewart fleet up to an adequate size to cope with passengers, freight and the mail for the next four years. All of the Stewart motor omnibuses were grey until 1926 when a Dennis 14–seat charabanc was added. It had a body by John Stewart & Sons — no relation — the Wishaw coachbuilders, and was blue. Although the green band which trimmed off the blue colour scheme cannot be seen in a contemporary postcard, the owner's name with the garter and 'S' are clearly visible, and this became the standard livery for the next decade. The Dennis was added to the fleet to cope with a demand for a South Arran — Whiting Bay service to replace the one operated by Hamilton, Kildonan. Several local people — and the Lagg Hotel — had asked Donald Stewart to provide a replacement service, and he did so, from Corriecravie to Whiting Bay via High Kildonan.

Another Dennis came in 1927; it had a destination indicator of sorts, so that roadside passengers could tell the Lamlash via Ross road omnibus apart from the Whiting Bay via High Kildonan vehicle. A little later in 1927 and subject to an agreement with the Gordon Bros. and Lennox operations, certain Stewart omnibuses were extended to Lamlash, although picking up on the way in and setting down on the way out restrictions applied over that section of route. Stewart and McNeill shared the road on a mutually-agreed basis between Whiting Bay and Dippen, at which point the two routes diverged.

In 1928 a brown FIAT 505–type six–seat tour car arrived. There were already several powerful six–seaters in use, and a 14–seat saloon coach, similar to the Lennox 'ice cream van', came the same year in time for the summer-only extension from Corriecravie to Kilpatrick and Blackwaterfoot.

By 1936 the Southern Garage had been built at Whiting Bay for the accommodation of three Bedford coaches of the WLB type which had arrived in 1931, 1933 and 1935. They were all 20–seaters, with coachwork by Alexanders, Bracebridge and Stewart of Wishaw. In the same year the route over the Ross road was discontinued, although tours were still operated over the road. The Ross road route had very few passengers, the south road was in better condition, but the main reason was that the Post Office introduced its own vans, and so did not need contractors to carry the mail to the remote parts of Arran any longer. A year later the blue-with-green-band colour scheme started to fade away (so to speak) when a 1937 model Bedford was delivered in white, with a green waistband and blue roof, thus setting the trend for the rest of the fleet from that date until the closure. The 1927 Dennis was next in line for retirement on the strict rotation basis which was the rule with Stewart's Motors and it went to a farmer in the North of England; he used it as a lorry for ten years after that.

The years 1939–41 were quiet. People were either away at the war or unwilling to travel — for holidays, that is; there was a steady stream of passengers — local people — for the reduced omnibus service, and by 1942, incredible though it may seem, Stewart's, and other Arran operators, found that there was a demand for some sort of tour from the small number of people who were able to come to the island. A second-hand Bedford 25–seater was found at Campbeltown, the first of the only two second-hand machines ever in the fleet. It was surplus to the requirements of the West Coast Motor Services, that ultra-smart family business which has served Kintyre, and provided the connection with MacBrayne's omnibuses to Glasgow over the Camp-beltown–Tarbert road for half a century. The West Coast company repainted it into Stewart colours (although the fleetname was left to Donald Stewart to apply), and it was loaded on to a steamer for Lochranza. Charles Weir, of whom more later, drove it to Black-waterfoot, and Donald Stewart Jr. took it on from there.

War-time omnibuses were not so frequent as those in the 1936–37 timetable. In fact, there were periods when there was only one departure each way in a day. Fares during the war years were:

Lamlash to Corriecravie	Single 2/6d	Day Return 2/9d
Lamlash to Blackwaterfoot	Single 3/-d	Day Return 3/6d
Whiting Bay to Corriecravie	As from Lamlash	
Whiting Bay to Lagg	Single 2/-d	Day Return 2/2d
Whiting Bay to High Kildonan	Single 9d	Day Return 1/3d

Period return fares from Lamlash were four shillings (20p) to Corriecravie and 4/6d (22½p) to Blackwaterfoot. From Whiting Bay the period return fare was three shillings (15p) to Lagg, and only 1/3d (6p), the same as the day return, to High Kildonan. These fares were kept at that level until several years after the Second German War, and the omnibuses returned to the same frequencies as those of 1936 and 1937.

At the end of the war many of Britain's omnibus fleets were in an appalling state due to lack of replacement/spare parts for machines which should have been scrapped at the start of or during the war. The Government allowed Bedford at Luton and Guy Motors at Wolver-hampton to build chassis with *strictly* utility bodies for companies which were desperate for new rolling stock. They had wooden seats. One of these, a second-hand Bedford 'Utility' omnibus was obtained in

1947 from Kia-Ora Motor Services of Morecambe, and the ex-West Coast machine was put on to the school run.

Although the Government was slightly quicker to demobilise the military at the end of the war than it had been to get them ready in the first place, it was 1946 before the High School (it was a Junior Secondary School in those days) was ready for the use its builders had in mind when it was finished in 1941. All schoolchildren over the age of 11, then and now, are 'bussed' from all parts of the island. The school at Lamlash was used by the Grey Funnel Line (Royal Navy) during the war, and the buildings (now the local council offices) at the other end of the village were still in use until then. By the end of 1946, the new school was ready, and 'Campbeltown Kate' as the scholars named the vehicle, spent the rest of her working life on the Corriecravie – Lamlash run. She was, as we've seen, a 25–seater (the sort of vehicle for which the school gateposts — which are still in place — were said to be too narrow), and her regular passengers decorated her inside surfaces with photographs of their favourite singing and film stars. All that is left of Campbeltown Kate now is the glass display screen from the back panel-top, and the front roller blind and mechanism. She was dismantled in 1976.

In 1947 two Bedford OB coaches were ordered with 29–seat Duple bodies. These were allocated the numbers SJ1081 and SJ1082, and the first of them —' 81 — entered service with Stewart's in 1947. It was 1949 before '82 arrived. 1081 was driven by Wee Jock MacDonald, by whom you could set your watch, and who was "never in an accident that he had caused himself".

In 1951 the fleet reached its peak with 11 touring cars, six omnibuses and coaches and two garages. There were daily tours:

ROUND ARRAN — 6/-d (30p).
STRING ROAD & SOUTH 4/-d (20p)

and evening tours:

CENTRAL ARRAN (ROSS & STRING ROADS) 3/6d (17½p)
ROSS GLEN & SOUTH END 2/6d (12½p)
MYSTERY TOURS AS ADVERTISED

The Gordon Bros. (ex-McNeill) interests at and from Kildonan were taken over in 1951, thus making Stewart's Motors *the* South

Arran company. When the motor car came, it pushed hard, and in 1960 the entire business was sold to Bannatyne Motors of Blackwaterfoot. The garages at Corriecravie and Whiting Bay were not required they were sold separately; and only three vehicles, SJ1081, 1082 and one other were included in the sale, the others became farm sheds or were dismantled. Once again, the South Arran omnibuses changed colour, this time to green.

The gates at either end of the one-way system road serving Brodick Castle bear a legend. In the case of the North gate the legend is "THROUGH" on either gate, with a heraldic device. The South gate also bears heraldic devices, but has the legend "NE OUBLIE" on one gate, and "THROUGH" on the other. When asked why this was, driver Bruce Hough said that the legend on the south (exit) gate was Latin for "NO ENTRY".

SHISKINE, LAGG & SOUTH COAST RAILWAY
Shiskine—Blackwaterfoot—Lagg—
Bennan Head Tunnel—Kildonan—
Dippin Shore—Whiting Bay

I'll grant you that the title of this chapter is drawing the longbow a bit but it so happens that a Light Railway to which the above title could have been applied was seriously considered in 1919, and formed part of the *Report of the Rural Transport (Scotland) Committee 1919,* p.164 on. This was a very impressive document, lavishly-illustrated with coloured maps and things, as well it should have, since it was formally laid before (according to its title page) not just the Houses of Parliament, but the King as well.

The Committee responsible for this report (sometimes known as the Geddes Report of 1919) went charging about all over the country looking at the Scottish rural areas and taking local advice and comment on new roads, railways, motor omnibus services (listed and shown as projected motor routes). Among the suggestions were a line of road across the Kintyre peninsula from Carradale to Tayinloan; a re-scheduled and re-routed steamer service between eastern Kintyre and western Arran, and — the light railway. It is clear, reading between the lines of the report, that in Arran, at least, the investigators relied a little too heavily on the opinions of a local and self-elected group of people — rather like the present day Community Council, perhaps — who, to complete the comparison, were not fully aware of what was happening in their area.

The Rural Transport (Scotland) Committee recommended that a line of railway should be built in the island after considering evidence laid before them and, one assumes, after coming here to see for themselves. At that time the east coast of Arran had a good service of steamers to and from the Clyde Coast, at Whiting Bay, Lamlash and

Brodick where goods storage and interchange facilities were established. The only pier on the west coast of Arran was at Lochranza, after which the steamers went to Carradale and Campbeltown. It was said that even if the rowing boat connection could be replaced by piers at Pirnmill and Machrie, with an additional pier at Blackwaterfoot, the steamer company was not in a position to make scheduled stops at them between Loch Ranza *(sic)* and Carradale. Since, as will be mentioned later, the absence of an 'adequate' steamer service *on the west coast of the island* was one of the reasons put forward and accepted for a Light Railway, it is astonishing that the eventual report specifically pointed out that "no extension (from Blackwaterfoot) would be necessary beyond Machrie", and even more amazing is the road across the Kintyre Peninsula being included in The Plan since, without pier/railway interchange linking Blackwaterfoot and Carradale, the Glasgow–Arran–Kintyre–Islay route as projected in the Report had a vital link missing.

The Report stated that the south of Arran had a population of 1,000, with "the Shiskine area about the same", and that exports from the area covered by the projected light railway were potatoes, sheep, cattle, pigs, wool, hay, seed and cheese; and that imports included 1,000 tons of coal, 700 tons of *artificial* manure and 1,000 tons of general commodities. (These figures were in respect of annual transactions, and the emphasis on several words and phrases above were inserted by me, not the Committee). The Report forecast an increase in exchange of the above-listed items, and visualised development of tourism, early potatoes, granite quarrying, stock, small farm produce, the woollen industry and afforestation in south and west Arran as a result of the light railway which would, in any case, "be viable without them".

Mention was made of "Mr. Colin Currie's motor service in another part of the island" and its benefit, in the main, to passengers (as opposed to goods), but none of the south Arran omnibus operators' motor omnibuses was mentioned; ignoring something in the hope that it might go away is not a new attitude!

The reason for a projected light railway and the reason that 'they' hoped that the motor omnibus (and lorries) might go away were one and the same; the roads at that time were simply not equal to the task of supporting heavy motor traffic. Although "stone or concrete channels (in

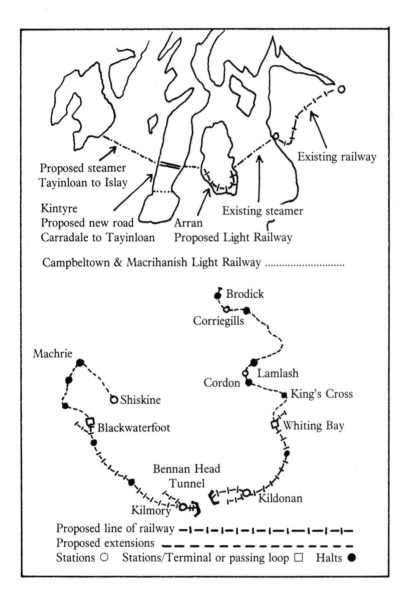

Proposed steamer
Tayinloan to Islay

Kintyre
Proposed new road
Carradale to Tayinloan

Existing railway

Arran
Proposed Light Railway

Existing steamer

Campbeltown & Macrihanish Light Railway ....

Brodick

Corriegills

Machrie

Shiskine

Blackwaterfoot

Cordon

Lamlash

King's Cross

Whiting Bay

Bennan Head
Tunnel

Kilmory

Kildonan

Proposed line of railway —ı—ı—ı—ı—ı—ı—ı—ı—ı—ı—ı—
Proposed extensions
Stations ○   Stations/Terminal or passing loop □   Halts ●

the road) to support the wheels of heavy tractors" was a notion which was given space in the report, the fact is that a light railway would have been only marginally more expensive to construct than an equivalent distance of Arran road would have been to up-grade, and when the higher maintenance costs of an up-graded road were taken into consideration, the light railway came out the winner.

It is necessary to digress here, for a few paragraphs, and establish just what is meant by the expression 'Light Railway'. The term usually conjures up an image of a tiny, narrow-gauge train such as the Campbeltown & Macrihanish Light Railway Company used, and running along a street, just as they did in Campbeltown (see Plate 15 & 16).

In fact, there are many factors which go towards making what we know as a Light Railway which can be, and often is, a standard gauge branch of an existing main line. The most important factors are: (1) Only one train 'in steam' on the line. That is to say, only one self-propelled vehicle or train, thus rendering signals unnecessary; (2) a maximum speed of 25 miles per hour; (3) no more than eight tons weight per axle per vehicle. So, although many Light Railways were narrow-gauge and ran through streets or along public roads, that alone did not make them Light Railways.

Like the one at Campbeltown, the railway planned for Arran had no connection with a main-line track, and so would not be bound to the standard gauge. it was planned as a narrow-gauge line — 2 ft. 6 in. — and as such would have been of a much lighter construction, and cheaper, than a standard gauge line. The initial project was for 18 miles of single-line track from Whiting Bay pier, along the coast past Dippen shore, to Kildonan, through a tunnel at Bennan Head, and along the shore to Kilmorie (sic). A siding was talked of at this point, presumably for storage and loading of wagons serving the creamery. There is no question, however, of it running to the creamery, since the gradient would be too steep. The line was to have continued on to a point near what is described as "Shiskine" but this could have been anywhere from Kilpátrick on to Blackwaterfoot and/or inland to a point near to the Hamilton Arms Hotel.

Had the line been built, and pre-supposing many other 'might have beens' the possibility of extensions are endless. The land required for the initial 18-mile line would have been purchased compulsorily, and it is worth bearing in mind that a company, if any, (it might have been government-operated) would have had trouble persuading the land-owners concerned to sell land for extension, since they were at that time, literally, feudal overlords, a position from which they are gradually being separated, to the obvious chagrin of some of their agents. Extensions from Whiting Bay to Lamlash and even to Brodick were allowed for in the Report, although since that part of the island was well furnished with the facilities which, lacking in south and west Arran, made the whole thing necessary at that time, this is surprising.

From an engineering point of view the line could have been extended easily from Brodick to Corrie or Sannox, and from Black-waterfoot to Lochranza, although even if the basic 18 miles had been built, and the conditions of the 1918–19 period remained unchanged, it does not appear that the extensions would have been economically viable.

In the event, of course, the conditions existing in 1918–19, when the Report was put together, changed very quickly, and the piecemeal reinforcing of the existing roads in south and south-west Arran, literally as the 'new' motor omnibuses and lorries fell through them, kept the way open, after a fashion, until 1929 when a Roads Authority was set up to up-grade the roads. It is not often that a railway proposed for an area is taken so far along the planning stage as this one was, and then finds itself shelved due to competition which has sprung up overnight, but that is what happened in this case. Had the investigation into the current conditions extended even so far as a discussion with Johnny Anderson at Pirnmill, his stated intention to open a motor carriage agency, together with the enthusiasm already being shown by some of his potential customers, might have led the Committee to suppose that Arran's section of 'The Plan' could have been dealt with, as it was elsewhere, by the blue broken lines on the accompanying map which denoted a planned Road Motor Service.

Against this, it must be considered that the Light Railway, while anticipating passenger traffic, was planned with freight in mind. Had it been built on that basis anything could have happened. It could, for instance, have been run at first as a freight-only line, like the original Stockton & Darlington Railway, with hurried additions to the rolling stock to accommodate passengers, or it might have been run for passengers and freight on alternate days, as the Bodmin & Wadebridge Railway was. Incidentally, the Bodmin & Wadebridge Railway was the first railway company in Britain to advertise and run a day excursion. It was in 1845, and the advertised purpose was to watch a public hanging at Bodmin Jail!

Certainly, it would have had to come to terms with the influx of tourists, and having done so, would have generated its own traffic in the same way as the West Highland Railway did (and, happily, still does). And just as certainly, it would have been closed by now — or would someone have provided a link across the Kilbrannan Sound to link it with the C&MLR (closed in 1932) to provide a Clyde Coast to Islay route which would have survived to serve an age when tourist routes are fashionable?

It is amazing, isn't it, the speculation we can distil from a few paragraphs in a forgotten document suggesting an 18-mile Light Railway?

Arran Bus Shelter Graffitti:
> *Arran Coachmen on the road,*
> *proud as a troop of Lancers.*
> *One in Three had a PSV,*
> *the rest were a bunch of chancers!*

(1) The Brodick—Corrie road, 1904.

(2) Glen Rosa, 1906

(3) Pre-motor road in the King's Cross district

(4) The String Road, c.1949

(5) Post–1929 Bridge at Lamlash

(6) Brodick Pier, 1908

(7) Whiting Bay Pier, 1908

(8) A Gordon's Albion at Whiting Bay, 1932

(9) Brodick 1960s. Bannatyne Albion, Weir Commer, Ribbeck Albion, Ribbeck Commer TS3, Bannatyne Leyland Comet.

(10) ATT Fleet. Alistair Nicholson

(11) Currie horse brake at Shiskine, 1905

(12) Lennox hire carriage, c. 1911

(13) Hamilton's brake at Lagg, 1889

(14) Willie Currie's mail cart off its usual route,
above Lamlash, 1908

(15) Jamieson, Kildonan, 1909

(16) Stewart, Corriecravie, 1897

(17) CMLR urban operation

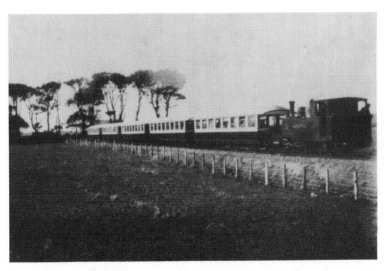

(18) What might have been CMLR rural operation

(19) The first motor car in Arran

(20) The first motor omnibus in Arran — Colin Currie's 1913 Albion

Post Office, King's Cross, Arran

(21) Bolt's 1918 GMC SJ222 at King's Cross c.1925 with George Moore and Maggie Smith behind McNeish's van

(22) Stewart's first T–Ford on the Ross

(23) Ribbeck's Albion 'Viking'

(24) Colin Currie's road-breaking Albion, 1925

(25) Made in Guildford, body fitted in Wishaw — Stewart's first
Dennis, a 14–seater, SJ521

(26) Lennox Chevrolet. On the back seat, in black, 'Greetin' Kate'

(27) Charabancs — probably McRae Brothers at Shiskine, c.1928

(28) A Ribbeck Albion 'The Valkyrie', with overflow starting tour

**(29) Hughie MacKenzie with McNeill Rolls-Royce
at Whiting Bay, c.1931**

(30) Gunboat Smith and (pre-Arran) McNeill Rolls-Royce

(31) Jimmy Anderson of Whiting Bay, charabanc c.1928

(32) A Robertson Thorneycroft on the way to Arran, 1930

(33) Two drivers with Stewart's 1937 Bedford WTB 25–seater

(34) John Hamilton, David Middleton, Ian Martin and Sam Ross
washing 14–seat Chevrolets in the burn, 1932

(35) Lennox Bedford Saloon

(36) Anderson's Berliet and McMillan's Ford at Pirnmill.

(37) 1931 Lennox Bedford

(38) 1931 Lennox Bedford

(39) Hammie Kerr with Silver Bullet

(40) Silver Bullet and passengers

(41) Weir's interchangeable Albion, 1934

(42) The 'new' Morris mail vans outside the —then— Post Office,
Brodick 1936/37

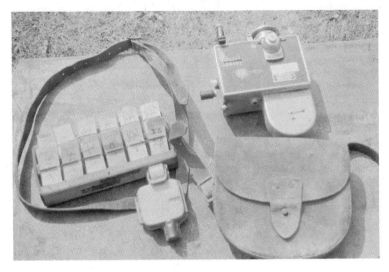

(43) Ticket rack and clipper, Setright ticket machine

(44) Ribbeck's 1937 Commer 'Avenger'

(45) Hamilton Kerr with a visitor — A. Lennox (son of Pa)

(46) Donald Robertson

(47) Bannatyne Motors Leyland Comet

(48) Lennox's Leyland Comet

(49) Bannatyne Motors Foden omnibus

(50) Lennox's Foden omnibus

(51) Ian MacKenzie with Lennox half-cab Leyland

(52) Ribbeck's half-cab Albion at Lochranza, 1961

(53) Lennox machines at Brodick, 607–AEC & 711–Foden

(54) Weir's 1947 half-cab Albion, known locally as 'The Train', with two Bedford's on the left, at Machrie

(55) Peter McMillan, Archie Currie, Colin Currie, Rab Hume, Nicol Currie, George Munro

(56) Hughie MacKenzie and friends

(57) McMillan Commer before sale to Lennox

(58) McMillan Commer after sale to Lennox

(59) Gordon's Albion, c.1938

(60) Bannatyne Motors Foden

(61) Douglas Kerr, the first motor-hirer in East Arran

(62) Many operators in Britain softened the rather spartan lines of the post-war 'austerity' vehicles by applying flashes, as Lennox has done here

(63) Weir's of Machrie Bedfords: 29-seat OB; 11-seat Dormobile

(64) Ribbeck's Morris 12-seat Minibus

(65) The Lennox depot, Whiting Bay, c.1929. The chap in the check
suit and hat at the door is no less a person than 'Pa'.

(66) The Lamlash garage, built by Ernest Bolt, shown here under
Lennox ownership

(67) John Smith and Elizabeth Arnott.   **Duncan Weir**

(68) Interchange at Lochranza, 1966

(69) A Lennox Albion, used for touring during the 1960s

(70) A Weir's Commer Avenger

(71) Bedfords on Ribbeck tour passing Bannatyne Foden omnibus, Machrie, 1966

(72) Three Scottish Aviation bodies, all built at Prestwick on to Albion chassis for delivery to various parts of Britain, ending their days at Blackwaterfoot.

(73) Two Ribbeck Bedford SBs, a Weir Commer and a Ribbeck Albion

(74) Lennox OB Bedford at Lochranza, 1966

(75) The ex-Devon General/Grey Cars Bannatyne Motors semi-automatic AEC Regal

(76) Lennox SB Bedford

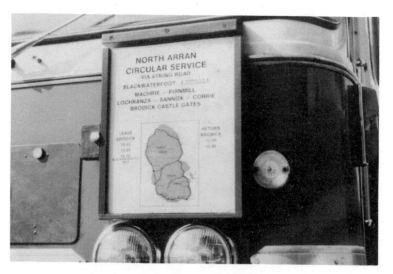

(77) **Supplementary route indicator fitted to
257, 258, 350 & 351 after 1979**

(78) **Dodge Postbus 716 at Brodick with driver John McBride**

(79) Land Rover Postbus at Blackwaterfoot

(80) Postbus No.319 at Blackwaterfoot with driver Alice Lennox

(81) Fergie Latona and Jack Lennox

(82) Donny Campbell

(83) Roy Dickie, Alice Lennox, Neil Kerr, Stuart Black, Donald McQueen, John McBride, Robert Gilligan, Billy Dickie.

(84) Louis Joss in Commer Postbus No.493 at Shannochie, 1979

(85) 947 — an ATT Bedford SB Bella Vega

(86) George McKechnie

(87) Danny Stewart in 139 at Whiting Bay. Winter 1981

(88) 16–seat Ford Minibus, Willowbrook body

(89) ATT No.400 — a dual purpose cuss or boach

(90) It never leaves the island

(91) The Old Grey Mare, ATT 783

(92) Frank Hamilton and Andy Lane.

(93) ATT 459 coming off the steamer

(94) The hired coach OPT594M, 1978

(95) **Passing, near Machrie 1982**

(96) **Phil Broomhead in 351 at Blackwaterfoot**

(97) Negotiating a Regional Council project that got out of hand at
Corrie (Asquith's 'prettiest village in Europe')

(98) Coming in to Arran High School, Lamlash — another tight
squeeze for Phil

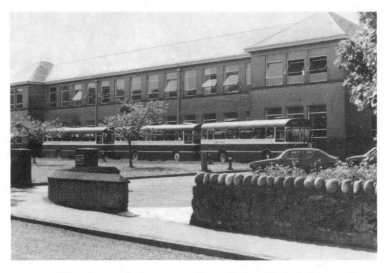

(99) The mass departure from Arran High School

(100) Andy Lane's Lamlash 'depot' — the car park in the White House woods, 1982

(101) Postbus No.717 climbing to Lavencorrach

(102) Coming down again

(103) Two visitors at the 'Community Arts' shelter,
Whiting Bay terminus, 1982

(104) The 'Wilkinson' shelter, with Marc Head comforting someone
who has just missed the bus

(105) Rear view of 138

(106) Rear view of 845

(107) Danny Craig

(108) Visitors to Arran each year for 40 years — Stan and Betty
Wyllie, with Elizabeth (less than 40 years)

(109) Grant Weir   Bruce Hough

(110) Danny Stewart

(111) Alistair Nicholson

(112) Alastair MacBride

(113) Ernest Gordon

(114) Bedford/Plaxton 45–seater driven by Alastair MacBride
at Brodick Pier, 1981

(115) Awaiting the morning rush, 1982

(116) Lennox's Brodick 'depot', c.1954

(117) The fact-finding committee: Jack Carson CDC, John Home-Robertson MP,
Albert McQuarry MP, David Lambie MP, Willie McKelvie MP,
Evelyn Sillars CDC, John Corrie MP, Richard Wilkinson SRC.

(118) Ralston Green, 1982

(119) Col. Currie, 1908   **Phil Broomhead, 1982**

(120) 53–seat Wright body on Bedford YNT
delivered 20th April, 1983. Driver Kevin Kilshaw

LENNOX, Whiting Bay. Lamlash. Brodick.
Whiting Bay — Kings Cross road-end — Lamlash — Brodick
Whiting Bay — Kings Cross
Whiting Bay — Largiebeg

It is difficult to establish the exact date when Lennox's first appeared on the scene as a passenger transport service. Mr. A.C. Lennox ('Pa') came to the island from Lanarkshire in 1902, just after the pier was completed, and it was shortly afterwards that he started to meet the steamers at Whiting Bay Pier with a horse-drawn carriage. In a remarkably short time he had several wagonettes, victorias and landaus for hire, all with drivers, and a machine known as a Governess Cart, which was almost certainly the first U–drive, or self-drive, in Arran. Hertz, Avis, Swan National, and even the Ayrshire and Glasgow firm of Mitchell Self Drive, while admittedly better-known to a wider public than Lennox was, are nevertheless a long way behind this remarkable man, who was a pioneer and innovator as well as an astute businessman.

The various horse-drawn vehicles were engaged in various activities around Arran; there were family outings, picnics, bathing, and most of Lennox's clientele came from the 'let' houses and from the hotels which were springing-up in the wake of the pier. Most of these hires were regular bookings pre-arranged from the initial pick-up at the pier, and subsequent trip to the summer residence of the family, through a picnic trip on Tuesday afternoons and a swimming party on Thursdays, to the eventual return at the end of the holiday to the pier. In addition, there were vehicles sent to meet each boat on a speculative basis, and in most cases the 'taxi' trip taking the family of visitors to their boarding house, let house, hotel or relative's house led to an arrangement whereby that coach and coachman would call at certain times on certain days to take the family on trips and excursions.

Pa Lennox purchased a large house nearly opposite the pier in Whiting Bay, and opened it as the 'Prospect Hill Private Hotel' with some stables at the rear for the accommodation of his animals and carriages. The animals in question were, one assumes, horses, ponies, and perhaps the odd dog or cat. Some years later when Sir Alfred Cooper built Cooper Angus House he became a regular client — and friend — of A. C. Lennox, and in addition to carriages, hired horses and ponies for the early morning rides of his guests.

The steamers to Whiting Bay came from several directions, went on, or returned to, several destinations, and were operated by several different companies, each of which was completely and totally at war with the others. Tales and stories are told by elderly people today of scenes which are said by them to have taken place in the 1940s, and while it is true that such scenes did take place, it was in the period 1880–1910 that most of the incidents took place. Such incidents, for instance, as a paddle steamer captain who would hold his ship alongside a pier on engines alone, spurning the use of ropes, while his passengers, who entered into the spirit of the thing, scrambled ashore, or aboard with no thought of dignity, care, or anything other than to arrive at their destination before the other ship. In the case of Glasgow & South Western passengers, 'the other ship' was of the Caledonian Steam Packet Company, and *vice versa*, although there were other competitors from time to time. There are recorded at the time, and by reliable unbiased witnesses, such incidents as the steamer of one company cutting across the bows of another to be first alongside a pier, and one newspaper even reported a case in which the passengers of the second steamer in had set about the Piermaster (they were, apparently, led by a local Baillie!) for allowing the other steamer into the pier before their own. In an age and circumstance where 'Hellfire Jack' and 'Captain Kidd' were commonplace nicknames, there were many steamer captains who were dashing to the point of foolhardiness, and any collision of a minor nature was more likely to cause a deputation of admiring passengers rather than disapproving Board of Trade officials.

Whiting Bay Pier was the only one in Arran which could accommodate two steamers at once, and although two competitors were never scheduled to arrive at that particular pier at the same time, they often did. Even at times when they did not, a steamer for Ireland was

A. C. LENNOX,
PIER GARAGE,
WHITING BAY.

Motor in Comfort, Luxury and Safety. Choose your Car from our High-Class Fleet of New Seven-Seaters with four-wheel brakes and experienced Mechanic Driver.

Patronise our True-to-Time Motor Coach Service between Whiting Bay, Lamlash and Brodick. Every Half-Hour in Summer, Twice Daily in Winter. Look out for the Red and Cream Coaches.

Splendid Garage Accommodation. Repairs by Expert Mechanics. Tyres, Accessories, Petrol and Oil Pumps, Electric Light Batteries Charged. Inspection invited without obligation.

Charges Strictly Moderate. Quotations Free.

Passengers and Third Parties Fully Covered by Insurance.

TO THE FESTIVAL—

On FRIDAY, 8th, and SATURDAY, 9th MARCH, COACHES will leave BRODICK at 11 a.m. and 2 p.m., LAMLASH 15 minutes later. RETURNING at 1 p.m. and at CLOSE.

A. C. LENNOX, Proprietor.
'Phone—Whiting Bay 10.

1929 advertisement

often alongside at the same time as one for Ardrossan, or further up the Clyde.

In the circumstances described, it will be realised that A. C. Lennox would not have thought highly of any of his drivers who mislaid luggage, or — worse — put it on the wrong steamer! In those days drivers were expected to carry luggage on to, or from, the steamer for their passengers and this is not intended to reflect on the taxi and omnibus drivers of today, in Arran or elsewhere; a passenger vehicle today with or without fairly large sums of money which cannot be left unattended is generally on a section of road which is required by other traffic. The only interest a passenger vehicle driver of today can have in the luggage of his passengers is in the length of time it takes for the passenger to find it, remove it and make way for someone getting on. Having said that, I should point out that, in general, Arran omnibus drivers try to — and coach drivers *always* do — assist where possible with loading and unloading of passengers' luggage from the vehicle, even though the days of shifting it from the steamer to the hotel and back are gone, except in the case (sorry) of the Scotia, National and other tours which start from the mainland.

All of which is a long way from the subject, to wit, Whiting Bay in the first decade of the 20th century, when the horse-drawn carriages with four, five and six seats for families were jostling for space with the 10 and 15–seat three-horse charabancs which carried individuals and groups who were unconnected with each other.

The Great War — 1914–1918 — took men and horses from the island, many never to return. It was a period of reduced services of both steamers and omnibuses, but by 1920 things were as nearly back to normal as anything could be in a country after a long war.

The omnibus service which had been tried tentatively as early as 1910 remained horse-drawn; with a fast and frequent shipping service on hand, travel from Whiting Bay to Lamlash and from there to Brodick was much quicker by steamer than by the rather primitive road on which there were few bridges over the many burns (streams) along the way. A motor charabanc was obtained and tours were put in hand. The machine was an Albion with solid tyres and a canvas roof which took ten minutes to erect. It must have been a spartan vehicle by today's standards. By 1924 it had been sold to Hamilton, Kildonan,

and several new motor charabancs had been obtained. The steamer
service had undergone amalgamation and rationalisation the previous
year, and a great deal of the wasteful competititon was done away with;
even though it meant that there were fewer steamers plying between
Brodick, Lamlash and Whiting Bay, the motor omnibus was coming
into its own, and as each year passed the newer models became more
and more reliable, and, of course, less primitive.

The visitors to the Isle of Arran, and particularly to Whiting Bay,
wealthy middle-class families with servants and an entire summer to
spend in the island, were disappearing, and a new type of visitor, the
day-tripper and the regular same-fortnight-same-place-every-year
visitor were the new customers for Arran's tourist facilities. There
were still wealthy families of the Edwardian middle-class type coming
to Arran, of course, but the 'ordinary punter', no stranger to the island
in smaller numbers, and in other places, started to flock to the east side
of the island from Glasgow, from Ayrshire, from most of the Clyde
coast, in fact, and later from farther afield. Motor charabancs were
used as omnibuses and for tours. The style of the mystery tour has
been described in the chapter devoted to Gordon Bros., Lamlash, but
A. C. Lennox knew how to keep the customer coming back for more —
even if it was more of the same — and he had his regulars and
adherents just as his rivals did. By 1928 there weren't too many rivals
left in and around Whiting Bay. Marion Sillars, Daniel Murray, Peter
Nicol and others had taxis and hire cars in the 1920s and Lennox had
some stiff competition in that respect, but the omnibuses and tour
coaches were confined to a handful of others — Gordon's, Anderson
and Kerr, with whom Pa was well able to hold his own.

Ernest Bolt's Lamlash garage was purchased in 1935, and although
Pa Lennox was neither childish nor mean, he may well have derived
some satisfaction from opening a depot next door to his rival, and deep
in that rival's territory, particularly in view of the way in which the
McNeill takeover had been effected, and to say nothing of the
impertinence of a Gordon Brothers booking office almost opposite the
Lennox garage in Whiting Bay.

The omnibus service fares, common to Gordon's and Lennox at this
time, were:

Whiting Bay to Lamlash 1/3d (6p)
Whiting Bay to Brodick 2/6d (12½p)
Lamlash to Brodick 1/6d (7½p)

The fare of 1/6d between Lamlash and Brodick was reduced to 1/3d in 1939. Neither Mr. Donnie Lennox or Mr. Ernest Gordon could recall the reason for this, although they said that it resulted in a small saving in ticket printing costs.

At one time in the 1930s there was a motor car in the Lennox fleet which has passed into legend and, like most legends, may have been exaggerated over the years. The machine in question was known as *The Silver Bullet* and changed hands several times. It was an open-top Buick, officially a six–seater, with a demountable canvas roof. Photographs elsewhere in this book show how many people could be packed into it. They were taken at the request of one of its drivers, 'Hammie' Kerr and illustrate a typical small touring party of the period.

The Silver Bullet is recalled as a 38 horse-power car, capable of climbing the Ross road in top gear. In an age when garage mechanics washed their overalls in a bucket of petrol, and used gallons of the stuff to clean down greasy floors (it was only 9d, less than 4p, a gallon), its return of only eight miles per gallon was not considered an important factor in the operating economics.

The visitor to Arran today, riding in air-suspended, pneumatic-tyred, shock-absorbed, air-conditioned, Dunlopillo'd, glazed and roofed comfort behind Dan Stewart or Donny Campbell on a smooth road will find it difficult to believe, but less than 60 years ago Lennox and other tour passengers thought nothing of piling out of a charabanc to help fill in a pothole, or to assist the driver change a tyre — and mend it at the next burn! There were more vehicles available at that time for 'on the spot' hires. Today's omnibus company cannot afford to have a £33,000 vehicle standing around just in case someone comes along with 45 friends and asks for a hurl round the island. In the 1920s it was a different matter. The vehicles carried only 20 passengers, there was always a casually-employed driver or two in the vicinity, and individuals and small groups did, from time to time, band together and ask about a charter, even though there were many tours in every possible combination and permutation on offer at various times of the day. A. C. Lennox, who had built the Pier Garage at Whiting Bay in 1924, added to it from time to time "as we needed the room", in the words of Mr. Donnie Lennox. As A. C. LENNOX & SONS the firm included:

SJ438 FIAT 14–seat saloon coach
SJ598 Chevrolet 20–seat omnibus
SJ614 Chevrolet 20–seat omnibus
GM5006 Buick four–seat taxi (second-hand from Glasgow)
GM5109 Buick four–seat taxi (second-hand from Glasgow)

and a six–seat Minerva motor car which, at 38 horse-power was a powerful machine. A Studebaker taxi and a Chevrolet 22–seat omnibus, which, with the Albion machines already mentioned, made up the Lennox fleet at the end of 1928.

The FIAT 14–seater, the first to have a fixed roof and forward entrance, was used with a Chevrolet 20–seater on the omnibus service between Whiting Bay, Lamlash and Brodick. The 14–seater had a large boot, known as the 'Drunk Tank', and was used for the last departure from Brodick at 10.30 p.m. in to Whiting Bay at 11 p.m.

In 1931, Bedford saloon coaches which, like the Chevrolets, were General Motors (GMC) products, started to appear in the Lennox colours which had always been maroon — later red — and cream, and indeed they became the backbone of most of the fleet from about that time.

The legend 'Lennox's' and the monogram of the initials A C L & S was taken off the sides of the vehicles, and a monogram of the initials of the new fleetname, 'Lennox Motor Services' was applied. Pa Lennox always denied — but never too strongly — that it was an attempt to encourage potential passengers that by riding in an LMS-marked vehicle they would be still in the hands of a well-known railway company. The LMS company on the mainland complained, but Mr. Lennox pointed out that he had been running a motor service, and using maroon or red and cream on his coaches and omnibuses for many years before the London, Midland & Scottish Railway had ever been thought of, let alone chosen its colours and initials.

The co-operation with Gordon Bros., Lamlash, as described in that chapter was in force by this time and one wonders if maybe Pa *was* trying it on a bit, but even if he was nobody blamed him. He was a hard businessman, but not an unscrupulous one. Indeed, he was one of the first of the few British omnibus and coach operators to pay the lodgings of imported drivers during the season, and only then when he could not find any room for them in one of his own establishments at no charge to them. This was told me by Mr. Hamilton Kerr, whose love for A. C. Lennox is such that even now, 50 years after, he keeps in touch with Pa's descendants. Lennox had some good ideas. He purchased a row of derelict cottages and demolished them, then used their cellars as inspection pits around which he built his garage. He was one of the first people in Arran to generate his own electricity, and he built and maintained the public hall at Whiting Bay. Wrack, seaweed and litter were cleared from the Whiting Bay beaches at the start of each season by Lennox's staff at his expense, and if one of them had to go to hospital in those days before the National Health Service, Lennox paid the bill, and usually donated a bit more to the hospital.

Services to King's Cross were tried, discontinued, and tried again. By 1938 it was uneconomic to send even a car, so the service was withdrawn completely and the hamlet is served by ordered taxis.

Sunday afternoon services were started and what a job *they* were to get started. There were objections at first, on religious grounds, but it is indicative of the changing world that two years later the Whiting Bay church minister asked Lennox Motors to provide a service for his parishioners who lived south of Glenashdale. An omnibus — it can truly be called that, since fares were levied to each individual passenger, 6d (2½p) — was laid on in 1947.

In 1947 King George VI, with his Queen, Elizabeth, now the Queen Mother, and with Princess Elizabeth (who is now Queen Elizabeth) and her boyfriend — as he was then — now the Duke of Edinburgh, visited the island. It was one of those family outings that Arran caters for. Now, it so happens that London Transport may *think* they know all there is to know about avoiding Royal Procession routes, and I will admit that they have got the practice of leaving Routemasters in the garages, or diverting them down side-streets, off to a fine art. However, Lennox's Motors were the people when it came to this sort of thing, even though they had not had any practice and it was a 'one-off' operation anyway. You will be aware, no doubt, that a chap from the

Palace staff goes round before a Royal visit, sorting things out — rather like those fellows in the Bible who used to go on before to 'make straight the way' before the King's feet. Now, bearing in mind that Arran in 1947 had very narrow roads and few cars, the whole thing was quite simple. The coach operators all agreed that no coaches would run in front of the procession, in either direction, before the Royal Family had left Brodick Castle, and taken a hurl down to the creamery at Kilmory, then on to Lochranza where a warship would be waiting to take them on to somewhere else. **Allister Craig Lennox**, son of Pa, noticed that neither he nor any of his competing coach operators had been asked to stay off the road *after* the Royal Family had passed. He did not discuss the matter with the other operators, but no sooner did the Royal Family pass his garage at Whiting Bay than a Lennox coach came up, complete with blackboard on which was chalked an advert for a trip to Lochranza with (or it might have been 'behind') the procession. Arran cannot field such a large crowd as London, but the crowd, such as there was, had not dispersed, and many of them took places in the Lennox coach, which had to be duplicated by more than one vehicle. This tale may serve to explain why, one day in 1947, Lennox's were the only coaches on the Arran roads and why three coachloads of Whiting Bay people were at Lochranza to see the King off!

The years between then and 1960 were the same for Lennox Motor Services as for other operators. Whiting Bay Pier was closed in 1957; Lamlash Pier had been closed three years earlier, partly as a result of the efforts of such men as Lennox, who, in providing a smooth, rapid and, no matter what the weather, reliable service between Whiting Bay, Lamlash and Brodick, had unwittingly perhaps persuaded travellers to enter and leave the island by the Brodick Pier. The two closed piers were, in any case, expensive to maintain, and the number of passengers using them wasn't thought by the Ministry of Transport to be high enough to prevent a Closure Order.

The introduction of the car-carrying steamers, purpose-built for the job was made in 1954. Until that time motor vehicles shipped to Arran had to make a rather hair-raising descent over the gap between the steamer and the pier, bridged by an improvised ramp. And this, mark you, after a voyage on an open deck. The new car-carrying steamers were slower to unload than had been supposed when diagramming the timetables for them had been considered. Even so, islanders were able to obtain motor cars from the mainland and the visitors were able to bring their own cars with them, thus reducing the number of passengers for omnibuses and tours.

There was still a demand for coaches; the Caledonian Steam Packet Company (the name retained by the companies combined into the LMSR in 1923, and nationalised and merged with British Railways in 1948) issued an excursion brochure in the late summer of 1957 which included:

> Brodick, Ribbeck's Motor 10.45
> Lochranza, steamer 11.05
> Campbeltown 01.40

Other details were given — the return times, and the fare, which was 9/9d from Brodick and six shillings from Lochranza, were quoted, but the interesting thing so far as this chapter is concerned is the footnote, which read:

NOTE:– Messrs. A. C. Lennox's Motor will, on certain dates, also provide through service from Whiting Bay and Lamlash to Lochranza to connect with the above sailing to Campbeltown. For details see local announcements.

There were other sailings from Whiting Bay that summer, the last one in which Whiting Bay had such a facility. They included a 6.25 a.m. departure to Ardrossan on Mondays. There were later ones on that and other days, and a direct sailing to Campbeltown at seven shillings return on Thursdays between 4th July and 29th August. Although Lennox's carried local passengers into Whiting Bay for the trips, the connection to Lochranza was a coach, as opposed to local omnibus run.

After operating the turn-and-turn about service during several winters, as described in the Gordon Bros. chapter, Lennox Motor Services found themselves at the start of the 1960s with: two omnibuses and one coach at the Brodick Pier Garage, taken over from Finlay Kerr-Newton; three omnibuses at the Lamlash Garage, and: four omnibuses and two coaches at the original garage in Whiting Bay. Pa Lennox had died some years previously and Donnie Lennox was in charge of the business, which also provided petrol, spares, repairs, to private cars; taxis; hire cars, and a haulage organisation — Currie's —acquired along the way.

In 1963 all of the Brodick interests were sold to the Arran Transport & Trading Co. Ltd., which operated its share of the omnibuses between Brodick and Whiting Bay in co-operation with Lennox Transport in the same way that Gordon Bros. Motors had in years gone by. Four years later, in 1967, the Lamlash and Whiting Bay interests were sold to A. T. & T., and Mr. Donnie Lennox retired.

ARRAN. 1928
"KNIGHT OF THE ROAD."

Photo by E. W. Tattersall, Brodick.

We have now at least one "Knight of the Road" in Arran. The well-known periodical, "News of the World," has inaugurated a Courtesy of the Road Campaign for motor drivers. Various acts of courtesy and consideration on the part of drivers are being reported to the paper by special representatives in all parts of the country, and drivers so reported are presented on application with the sum of one guinea and a medal. Mr Allister Craig Lennox, son of Mr A. C. Lennox, Pier Garage, Whiting Bay, who drives one of the Whiting Bay-Brodick 'buses, is the first Arran driver to appear in the "honours list," and we offer him herewith our congratulations

**ANDERSON, Whiting Bay
Tours**

Jimmy Anderson was a joiner turned car-hirer, with a fleet which consisted at first of just two Buick motor cars, which nevertheless gave a good deal of competition to A. C. Lennox and others from 1927 to 1930. Most of the journeys undertaken at first were taxi-runs to and from the pier at Whiting Bay, although there were some tours as well. The tours became the major part of the business at the start of the 1928 season, when two red charabancs (one of which was a Chevrolet) were added to the fleet.

Most of these tours were cut-price; Jimmy Anderson knocked 2/6d (12½p) off the price agreed locally among the other operators, and half-a-crown was not an insignificant sum in those days. It is said that he applied for an omnibus licence when the Traffic Commissioners sat at Brodick in 1930, but there is no record of this. In any case, the two charabancs were kept busy with tours, and if he had wanted to obtain an omnibus licence he would not have failed to put an omnibus on to the road in 1929, even though it might not have fared well in competition with Lennox and Gordon omnibuses, so that he could show an 'established route'. That he did not do so is a clear indication that he had no desire to run a scheduled stage carriage service.

All of his vehicles were overhauled regularly, and the way in which this was stressed when I was told about it leads me to suppose that he was extra-meticulous in this respect, since regular maintenance was the order of the day for most of the transport contractors in the area at that time. The drivers were responsible for the maintenance of their own machines, although there was a full-time mechanic to see to the less mundane tasks which arose. The drivers were also required to get out of bed early twice a week to roll the 45-gallon drums of petrol unloaded from the steamer to the garage. Great care had to be taken to ensure that the cars did not run out of petrol on a round-Arran trip. They were thirsty brutes, as Hamilton Kerr once told me, and in addition they only had ten-gallon tanks. Mark you, this was typical of most touring cars and charabancs of the day, and not peculiar only to the fleet of Jimmy Anderson.

After 1930 the two red charabancs disappeared. I can find no trace of either of them in any other Arran omnibus fleet after this date. The cars motored on, and at one time in the 1930s the *Silver Bullet* is said to have been in Anderson's possession, although I cannot establish if this was before or after having been in the Lennox fleet. As to Jimmy Anderson, I asked Hammie Kerr what happened to him, and the car fleet, to be told that he had "turned it in at the end of 1939", and that at that time the fleet had consisted of three Buicks, two Chevrolets and a 1929 Armstrong Siddeley saloon purchased second-hand "frae a Glesca punter".

A south Arran omnibus was rolling through the rural area round about Kilmory when a tractor came out of a field unexpectedly. In order to avoid the tractor the omnibus driver — who was going too fast to stop — swerved, jumped a ditch, crashed through a hedge and went round the field twice before stopping. One of the men on the tractor turned to the other and said: "We only just got out of that field in time."

BOLT, Lamlash
Lamlash—Kings Cross
King's Cross—Whiting Bay Pier
Lamlash—Brodick Pier

In addition to making history in Lamlash, Ernest Bolt can be said to have made geography as well. In 1925 or thereabouts he built the Central Garage at Lamlash. The building, which later passed to A. C. Lennox, has since been demolished, and a bar, restaurant and function room built by and for the use of Mr. Rodden Middleton, a local haulage contractor, now stands on the site, which is next to the garage built by Gordon's Motors, later owned by Arran Transport and now, still a garage, owned by Lamlash Automarine Engineers.

Ernest Bolt had a one-ton Ford, that ubiquitous dual-purpose lorry-cum-everything-else that Johnny Anderson was importing in great numbers through Pirnmill. He used this to transport the spoil from the excavations for the garage to the back garden of the house of Mr. Alexander 'Ching' Hamilton, J.P., the well-known Lamlash tailor. There were several hundred loads shifted before the back garden of Ching's house was level, and it was said by Ching that it was one of the best bargains he had ever struck at one shilling (5p) a load!

Ernest Bolt had several motor cars for hire from Lamlash Pierhead and from the garage,and as we have seen, a motor lorry. The vehicle shown on Plate 21 is a GMC, first licensed and registered (SJ222) to John Kerr, and purchased from Kerr in 1928. It was used by Ernest Bolt, as it had been by John Kerr, for the spasmodic service, mainly on request for King's Cross residents who preferred boarding the steamer from Lamlash or Whiting Bay Pier to embarking from an open boat off King's Cross Point. At other times it went to Brodick. There was, in addition, another charabanc, of which no details are known, save that it was kept busy with tours.

Ernest Bolt employed several local men, including his brother-in-law, Robert Dempsey, who ran the office side of the business and, when he left school, Ernest's son Archie joined the business.

The family were closely connected with the life of the village; Ernest had held a commission in the Scottish Rifles during the Great War, and was a life member of the Masonic Lodge, of which he was treasurer for many years.

In 1930 the garage, rolling stock and goodwill of the business were sold to A. C. Lennox and Ernest Bolt returned to Southampton, from whence he had originally come. He became a sub-postmaster shortly afterward and became Chairman of the Southampton branch of the Sub-Postmasters' Association, a position he still held at his death in 1946.

Climbing down from his cab to survey a German saloon car he'd just shunted, an Arran omnibus driver said, with a philosophical air: "That's the way the Mercedes Benz."

GORDON BROS. Lamlash, Kildonan
Whiting Bay—Lamlash—Brodick
Lamlash—Kings Cross—Whiting Bay
Kildonan—Whiting Bay—Lamlash—Brodick

When Johnny Anderson extended his business to cover the sale of motor cars there were many people in Arran anxious to obtain one, mostly to provide a taxi and/or hire service for the visitors who were flocking to Arran at the end of the Great War. James Gordon was one of Anderson's early customers. He purchased two model-T Fords and started in on 'car hires and tours'. After the first year of operation James became aware that the motor car was here to stay, and would be increasing to numbers undreamed of when the first ones were made available at Pirnmill. Accordingly, he left the car hire business in the hands of his brother, Ernest, while he went off to Detroit in the U.S.A., to learn something of the motor trade from the Ford Motor Company. He returned in 1924 and telephoned Ernest from Glasgow to say that he had obtained another motor car — a Talbot — and went on to say that from what little he had seen since his arrival back in Britain, motor omnibuses seemed to be the up-and-coming thing. Ernest replied that he had, in fact, arranged for a motor charabanc to be delivered, and that it was on its way to Arran.

Thus, shortly after James returned, the Gordon Brothers had a fleet consisting of the two original T-Fords, the Talbot acquired by James, a black and blue six–seat Ford tour car, SJ339 (originally registered to James Kerr in 1922 and purchased from him in 1924), a black five–seat Ford, SJ406 (registered new to James Knox in 1923 and obtained from him in 1924), a grey and black five–seat Ford, SJ429, new to Gordons in 1924.

The motor charabanc, SJ480, arrived early in 1925. It was a blue Chevrolet, and seated 14. The machine soon earned the name 'The

Pirate' since, in common with many mainland omnibus services, the Gordon Brothers had a habit of cutting-in on a rival omnibus (in this case the rival was the already established A. C. Lennox) and maintaining a lead of a few minutes all the way to the end of the route, which, so far as Gordons were concerned, was Brodick to the north and Whiting Bay to the south. The practice of dropping off passengers short of the destination and turning back to pick up a crowd waiting to travel the other way was not so common as it was on the mainland, but it did happen now and then. At other times the *Pirate* would cruise up and down looking for passengers. I should point out at this stage, for the benefit of younger readers, that this practice was not generally regarded as disgraceful (except, perhaps, by the established company), and that it was common throughout the British Isles in the 1920s. Many of today's mainland omnibus companies can trace their ancestry to practices such as I've described, and Gordons were by no means the worst offenders. Indeed, it was the regular activities of mainland 'pirate' companies, long after the Gordons had settled down to a regular service, which led to the provisions of the 1930 Road Traffic Act and its requirement that omnibuses were properly licensed and regulated.

By 1929 there was another vehicle in the fleet, a 14-seat sun saloon coach, SJ619, a blue and red Chevrolet; and in that year James Gordon purchased the Ship House at Lamlash for use as a residence by the family. The outbuildings were used to garage the vehicles until the garage was built, and a booking office was opened in Whiting Bay.

By 1930 the Gordon Brothers' omnibuses, private hires and tours were well established, the Traffic Commissioners Court which sat in Brodick to hear applications for, and objections to, licences granted a service licence to Gordon's between Whiting Bay and Brodick in competition with the service provided by Lennox. Apparently the two main contenders for the Brodick to Whiting Bay route, Lennox and the Gordon brothers, had come to an agreement to work together, and not to oppose each other's application, while at the same time, as the two oldest-established operators, opposing, successfully, the applications of any other party. This was common practice throughout Britain, and although the general idea of a 'one company monopoly' for any omnibus was a good one (take my word for it, please, since I am not going into it now, especially since the Act of 1980 has stood the whole thing on its head) it was, nevertheless, nearly impossible for the Traffic Commissioners of any area to decide between two long-established operators, and if they were in agreement they tended to license them both, subject to such conditions as they considered appropriate.

By 1930 regular services had been established and weekly, fortnightly and monthly tickets had been introduced. The fare from Brodick to Whiting Bay was two shillings (10p) at first, but this was

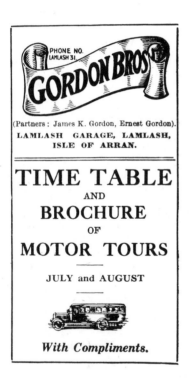
"The poacher turned gamekeeper" — Gordon's timetable (1934).

often undercut, either by Gordon's or by their rival, Lennox. Once the two companies came to a joint working agreement the fares were raised slightly and undercutting on the omnibus route became a thing of the past.

Right from the start Ernest and James had realised the value of advertising, and presented bulk consignments of 'Gordon's Motors' shaving towels to hotels and guest houses. A small 'Welcome to Arran' booklet was produced and distributed, and while it was of a general nature and available to anyone, Gordon's customers or not, an indication of omnibus times, coach tours and prices available from Gordon's Motors was well to the fore. The booklet described Arran as seen from a coach seat, and copies were available to anyone who cared to ask for one at just about any shop counter between Brodick and Whiting Bay. In later years these booklets were also available in smaller numbers to visitors in other parts of the island.

Word of mouth is as good a way of advertising as any, and certainly much cheaper. Furthermore, a good tale loses nothing in the telling. For this reason Gordon's Motors set out to give people something to talk about, and launched their mystery tours. You may wonder, as I did when Ernest first told me about them, where the 'mystery' lay, since a charabanc pointing 'down' the road could go only one way, and a charabanc pointing 'up' the road was similarly restricted by the very narrow choice of routes offered by Arran's road system. In fact, the mystery was not where the vehicle was going, but what would happen along the way. Sometimes the coaches would stop beside a field where a band was ready to play for dancing, and at other times the stop would be at any one of a half a dozen village halls in the island, where a 'Community Sing Song' or a 'Concert' was the entertainment. Tea, biscuits and sandwiches always formed part of the stop, and Ernest Gordon once told me that he was frying bacon at 1 a.m. on one trip, where 304 passengers were carried, necessitating re-hires from other coach operators. The sing-song was usually conducted by Ernest, with a stick of rhubarb for a baton. More often than not Ernest would stop the singing and point to someone in the hall, saying that he or she was not singing in tune. He would then make the person thus singled-out sing the verse again and again until he was satisfied. Ernest claimed to be tone deaf, but he certainly knew how to 'milk' a crowd for laughs.

Prizes were given for the best singer, the worst singer, or for any other reason Ernest thought. The prizes often took the form of small saucepans, and I met an elderly lady not so long ago who still cooks her porridge in a saucepan she won from Ernest on a Gordon's Motors tour. In her case the prize was to go to the occupant of seat 47 in a rather large hall. The numbers had been scrawled at random, and in no particular order, in chalk on the undersides of the seats, and the confusion attendant upon everyone standing up to look under their seats is something best left to your imagination, but this would have been nothing compared to the mock boos, catcalls and cheers which accompanied all prizewinners on their way to the front of the hall to receive their prizes, of which the most coveted, by the way, was the stick of rhubarb! This often went to a regular tour patron known as 'Greetin' Kate'. She was never known to have joined in the singing and, while she was a pleasant sort of lady, she seemed oblivious to surrounding scenery or noise and concentrated on her knitting.

Nowadays the thought of shifting 200 or 300 tour patrons does not seem to be a great problem, with 45– and 53– seat vehicles being so commonplace, but in the 1920s and 1930s a 20-seater was the more or less standard size. Add to this the problem of maintaining a frequent service on the omnibus route and the demand for seats on competitors' tours, and you will see that utilisation of existing vehicles and re-hire of competitors' vehicles was a delicate art. Further, with tea and sandwiches expected at each stop, careful timetabling had to be worked out, particularly when other tours necessitated the use of more than one of the smaller halls.

The red and blue Chevrolet SJ619 which had joined the fleet in 1929 was joined in 1930–31 by two more 14–seat Chevrolets, SJ648 and SJ687. These set the pattern for the Gordon Bros. livery which, after 1931, was dark blue, red and light blue, with a gold stripe and gold lettering.

The omnibuses ran from Whiting Bay to Brodick village, then back to Brodick Pier, with the return journey starting at Brodick Pier and terminating at the pier at Whiting Bay. The first 'run-outs' of the day were in each direction from the garage at Lamlash, with the last departure from Whiting Bay running to Lamlash only. (The last departure from Brodick was operated by Lennox and went through to

Whiting Bay). In common with most island omnibus services, Gordon's carried 'messages' and medicines to most houses (or collection points) along the route. They were delivered to the omnibus by an agent from whom they had been ordered, and dropped-off where required. Spools of film were also uplifted and collected in this way, or given to a conductor for delivery to, and collection from, a commercial photographer in Brodick to whom Ernest's wife, Kate Currie — one of the most beautiful girls in Arran, then and now — had been apprenticed.

The service frequency intensified during the late 1930s and the 1940s, aside from the Second German War years. This is a good point at which to remind younger readers that there were not so many cars around then as there are now, and further, that mainland resident visitors to Arran who did have cars could not bring them into the island so easily as today, since there was no roll-on-roll-off steamer. Gordon's and Lennox's between them provided three departures an hour each way on the Brodick to Whiting Bay route, with interchange of tickets, so that a person boarding a Lennox omnibus at Whiting Bay purchasing a return ticket could use that ticket to return from Lamlash· or Brodick on a Gordon's omnibus, and *vice versa*. This was not an amalgamation. The two omnibus services were separate from and independent of each other they merely found it convenient to themselves and to the travelling public to work in co-operation and co-ordinate their omnibuses. Competition for private hires and tours between the two companies was a different thing,however, and came to little short of all-out war. The rival Lennox service had its own version of the Gordon's tours already mentioned, and it was by no means unusual for the goodwill generated by an evening tour to spill over to the omnibus side of the business, when patrons of a Gordon's tour would stand back from a Lennox omnibus next morning to wait for a Gordon's vehicle. This partisanship, while not universal among visitors who wanted to travel by omnibus, was by no means unusual and, of course, Lennox Tour patrons who had enjoyed themselves the night before would wait for a Lennox omnibus.

I cannot see it happening today. Most people come to Arran in their own cars to "take things easy" then attempt to break their own and other people's necks in their hurry to get from one part of the island to the next, and with the excuse ever-ready — if needed to explain an accident — that "they did not know the road". Truly, we live in a different age.

In 1935 the service and tours, *and* vehicles, of McNeill, Kildonan were taken over in the circumstances described in the McNeill chapter. I do not know how the secrecy was maintained; presumably (but knowing Ernest as I did, I'd say that it was not certain) the Traffic Commissioners had been advised of the intended takeover; and if so, I can only assume that Pa Lennox did not have a regular order for 'Notices and Proceedings'. Whatever the case, Gordon's acquired an edge over their rival in that they had a ready-made extension to their existing route, and a pair of vehicles which were in themselves an attraction. No doubt Pa Lennox had the same feelings at that particular moment towards the Gordon brothers as the Great Western Railway had towards the Midland and the South Western companies when they took over the Somerset & Dorset Railway, but unlike the GWR, Lennox's was run by a man who, although as sharp as the next, knew how to behave like a gentleman, and as such made very little fuss about what he could well have felt justifiably aggrieved.

The extension to Kildonan was usually taken up by a vehicle coming into Whiting Bay from Brodick (a Gordon's vehicle, of course) but there were times when a run to Kildonan was made by a vehicle starting from Whiting Bay. Under the Gordon's regime, as had been the case under McNeill ownership, these runs were timed to connect with a Lennox omnibus, and great care was always taken to ensure that the Kildonan-bound vehicle did not leave before the one from Brodick arrived and transferred passengers. Through booking to and from any point between Kildonan and Brodick was available only on a Gordon's omnibus, the interchange of tickets arranged for the Whiting Bay to Brodick route still held good between those places, but passengers from Lamlash or Brodick for Kildonan could book right through only if they were on a Gordon's vehicle. On a Lennox omnibus, it was necessary to re-book when on the Kildonan omnibus to which the passengers changed at Whiting Bay.

There are stories handed down, relating what happened when two companies disagreed in the 1920s and before. The Cambrian Railway thought nothing of sending one of its trains away from Whitchurch station if the London & North Western Railway, with which it was quarrelling, had a delayed connection, and the Great North of Scotland Railway used the same tactic when in dispute with the Caledonian Railway. It seems to have been common business practice. It was not the practice of Pa Lennox to indulge in such tricks; although he may well have been annoyed at the way in which the McNeill sale went through against him, he was most insistent that Lennox omnibuses leaving Whiting Bay for Brodick should not do so if the connection from Kildonan was delayed. With a 20-minute service from Whiting Bay I imagine that he drew the line after five minutes or so, but the fact is that he did try to maintain any scheduled connection.

Gordon's Motors — as they were known by then — ran a spasmodic service from Lamlash to King's Cross during the late 1930s. The King's Cross Services in general are dealt with in a later chapter insofar as I can sort them out, but the Gordon service seems to have started as a scheduled once-a-day run, then deteriorated for want of passengers into an 'as required' trip, using the Talbot touring car, and finally to have been discontinued in 1938.

The shortage of petrol and spare parts during the Second German War necessitated a severe reduction in the omnibus services and tours were out of the question. When petrol was available a coach was hired by Lamlash residents for a trip to a dance at Lochranza or elsewhere, and on such occasions, the coach would return 'the other way round' when there was little or nothing in it in terms of mileage. Most of the Chevrolets so popular in the late '20s and early '30s had gone from the island omnibus fleets. Gordon's had only one of them left in service. Several new Bedford WLB saloon coaches, seating 20 and 25, had been put into service in 1936 and these were the mainstay of the fleet until long after the war. One of the utility body Bedford OB types was obtained in 1946 after which things started to improve, with petrol becoming much less scarce and village dances being revived, thus leading to extra work again in the evenings for the coaches. School contracts were tendered for and won, and although the practice developed during the war of utilising 'quiet' omnibus runs to and from Whiting Bay or Brodick for tours was continued in the form of cheap off-peak returns, the business returned to a near-enough pre-war level by 1949, when the new Duple bodied Bedford OB type saloon coaches arrived.

By 1951 the end was in sight. The ex-McNeill Whiting Bay to Kildonan service was handed over to Stewart's of Corriecravie in that year, and the number of passengers on the Brodick to Whiting Bay route started to fall off. By the mid-1950s it was clear that the route would not support two operators, so the winter service was put on to a three-month turn-and-turn-about basis, with Gordon's operating the second three-month period. In the spring of 1960 the entire Gordon's Motors business was sold to Lennox's.

One of the early mailcart drivers mislaid a postcard addressed to a house on his round. "I am sorry," he said to the householder, "but it was only from Flora saying she was having a good time in Perth, and she will be back on Saturday."

CANNON, Lamlash
"The man who carries the packman, carries the pack"
Colin Currie 1849–1919

Old Col was right, of course, but the maxim he had handed down can apply only to the average 'packman'. The Isle of Arran, 'Scotland's Holiday Island', has been a tourist resort for 100 years, and the packman's requirements have changed somewhat in that time. One of the most prominent features of the Arran holiday trade is the number of holiday houses in the island. Today, a holiday house is generally a dwelling owned by a mainland resident for use at weekends and in the summer. There is a surprisingly large number of these — surprising because I have not yet met a District or Regional Councillor who denies being against the use of houses in this way, when local people cannot compete with the high prices demanded, and thus have to spend a long time on a council house waiting list.

The holiday houses to which I refer in this context are houses owned by local people. Many of these houses had small cottages in their back gardens, to which the house owners would retire during the summer, leaving the main house free for use of regular visitors. There are still some of this type of holiday house about in Arran, and very difficult to get into by virtue of their popularity. Many of them have regular bookings from families who always come for, say, the first two weeks in June, and vacate the house in time for another family who always come for the second two weeks, and so on. I have heard it said that the only way to get a holiday house booking in such cases is to inherit one!

In the 1920s there were many of these houses with the 'back house' occupants providing various services or none at all, depending on the requirement of the visiting family. Many visiting families took a house for most of the summer — a practice which was common in the period

1880—1929, but this is a style of holidaymaking which has now died out. The families which came on this basis were usually well-off, and they spent the entire summer here, with 'Papa' catching the first steamers in the morning from the island. This would enable him to be in his office by 0900 (or just after) and he could be back in the island by 1800 after a day's work. The families of this class came to Arran accompanied by servants, and encumbered by trunks and hampers containing clothes, bed-linen and all sorts of other things such as crockery and cutlery. The families were met at the pier and conveyed to their house by pre-arrangement with one of the carriage hirers, who often catered for their transport for the entire summer. A. C. Lennox was one of the most popular contractors, although there were many others. The big problem was that very few of the carriages which had, of course, been constructed for the conveyance of passengers could cope with the luggage as well, even when it was sent in advance. So local 'general hauliers' were called-in to deal with this side of the transport arrangements.

One of these general hauliers was Charlie Cannon. He was not the earliest recorded haulier — indeed, he appears on the scene at a late stage in the era which I have described, but he became one of the best known, and certainly one of the best remembered of the carters. In addition to carrying the luggage for the visitors he undertook the removal of coal from the puffers so his men and his vehicles were seldom far from the piers at Lamlash and Whiting Bay.

Charlie Cannon started his business in the early 1920s and within a few years had expanded it to include several motor lorries. They had solid tyres — one of them is said to have been a steam-Foden — and like all of his subsequent motor lorries, they were painted blue with a red stripe, a company colour scheme which was reflected on the doors of his depot at Laigh Lettre, Lamlash, and on the petrol pump, one of the first, after McBride's, in Arran. He had always wanted to be a farmer; his interest in agriculture and animal husbandry was deep-seated and lifelong. He may well have satisfied it to a certain extent by the association he had with many of the island's farmers who looked to him for the carriage of livestock and produce to the mainland, and implements and machinery to the farms.

As the age of mechanical farming and the age of the motor car gathered momentum, the age of the family servant died. The big houses had fewer summer visitors of the type we have seen, and Charlie, who had often worked until past midnight with his drivers loading trunks and hampers now found himself busy hauling 'tarry metal' from the puffers to the road gangs who were busy upgrading the roads at the end of the 1920s.

Charlie retired in 1939 to Oakbank, although 'retired' is a relative word, since Oakbank was a farm. Charlie was at last where he wanted to be. The business was handed-over to his brother, Jimmy Cannon, and in addition to several motor cars for tours and private hire, there were no fewer than six lorries, all busy. The years during the Second German War were a bit of a headache for Jimmy Cannon. Omnibuses and coaches could be cut back to minimum timetables, starved of petrol and spares, and people could be asked "Is your journey really necessary", but farm transport had to go on as before, with reduced allocation of petrol, sympathy instead of spares, and, to make matters worse, a Naval Establishment set up, with all its attendant demands — on Jimmy Cannon — for transport of stores and equipment. Jimmy's sister, Grace, often drove one of the lorries, and between them, with help from a reduced staff (many of Arran's drivers had gone to war) they managed to cope. I once asked Grace if it had been very difficult. She thought for a moment, then said, "Well, we won, didn't we?" She was a remarkable lady.

At the end of the war the lorries were gradually replaced. There were still only six, and one of these was used on the dustbin round. It is the practice in parts of Scotland for local authorities to invite local contractors to tender for the refuse collection and disposal contract, a practice which, as far as I know, is followed in England only at Southend-on-Sea, Essex, and then only recently.

And what about the 'packmen'? These were the lighthouse keepers at Pladda Lighthouse. The lighthouse is on Pladda, a very small island just off Kildonan, but the keepers, when ashore, live at the Shore Station at Lamlash. Jimmy Cannon had the contract from the Northern Lighthouse Board to carry all mail, supplies and keepers to and from the beach at Kildonan, from where a small boat took them out to the lighthouse, and brought the off-duty keepers, who had been thus relieved back to Lamlash, a distance of some eight miles. Jimmy

Cannon died in 1963 and the requirements of local farmers were met after that by other local hauliers. The lighthouse contract remained in the Cannon family, and Grace continued to carry the keepers and their packs between Lamlash and Kildonan — I was one of them for a time — until her death in the mid-1970s, after which a nephew, Mick Cannon, took it over.

Although Rolls-Royce Motors were not particularly pleased when they heard that the Ranken Brothers tour operation in Glasgow had converted some Rollers to 14- and 16-seat charabancs, they had more or less got over it by 1936 when two of the machines had found their way to Arran and on to a Gordon Bros. omnibus route. It is said that a Rolls-Royce company official was on holiday in Arran in 1937 and that he got into conversation with Ernest Gordon. He asked after the two Rollers and Ernest told him that they were very pleased with them. All you could hear, when the motors were running, was the ticking of the clock on the dashboard. The Rolls-Royce chap blushed and shuffled his feet, then said: "We have been trying for years to do something about those bloody clocks."

THE KING'S CROSS OMNIBUSES
King's Cross—Whiting Bay Pier
King's Cross–Lamlash Pier

Most of the districts and villages in Arran are on roads which lead to somewhere else. In addition they had only one — sometimes two — , operators whose routes and times were such that a complete start to finish record is easy enough to establish. The area and hamlet known as King's Cross is a different matter entirely, since it is on a side road which does not lead to anywhere else, and since the activities of the operators serving it tended to overlap. So, although the activities of some of the operators listed in this chapter are also looked at in the chapter dealing with them, a brief account of the services to and from King's Cross may not come amiss.

The first recorded visitors to, and departures from what is now known as King's Cross are said to have been travelling to Arran as early as 3000 BC, and the Vikings left tangible evidence of forts, in the 9th century AD. King Robert the Bruce is said to have set off from, and given the name to King's Cross after travelling from the cave with the persistent spider, which is said to have been at Blackwaterfoot. He was awaiting a signal from the Ayrshire mainland and crossed when he mistook a fire started by accident by some drunken English soldiers for a pre-arranged signal from his own supporters.

For the purpose of this particular history we can miss the first 5,000 years and take as our starting point the year 1880. It was in that year that the paddle steamer *Ivanhoe* was launched by Henderson & Co. at their Partick yard to the order of the Firth of Clyde Steam Packet Company Ltd., a syndicate which included a director of the Allan Line, a director of the City Line, a Captain —James Brown — of the City line and Captain James Williamson. The *Ivanhoe* was a 'temperance' boat and an extract from the prospectus of the Company reads:

> *"..... to provide an all day sail without the liability of witnessing the disorderly conduct ... usual on river steamers, and to exclude persons unable to enjoy a holiday without getting drunk, creating disturbance ... etc."*

Ivanhoe sailed from Helensburgh, unlike other steamers, and her route took her to Greenock, Gourock, Dunoon, Wemyss Bay (where there was a connection made with the Caledonian Railway, into the fleet of which she was eventually taken) and on to Rothesay, Isle of Bute, then to Arran. She laid off Corrie while a rowing boat connection transferred passengers, steamed on to Brodick where a pier had been built in 1872, then proceeded to Lamlash. Here, until 1883, a rowing boat connection was provided, after which date a pier was completed. From Lamlash she went on to Whiting Bay with an intermediate stop off King's Cross, to where we shall return just as soon as we've seen it down to Whiting Bay. It was here that she turned back after landing passengers by rowing boat, until 1901 and on to a pier built by that date.

King's Cross was a port (or, at any rate, a point) of call on every journey the *Ivanhoe* made, once a week in 1880 and 1881, then every day from 1883 to 1889, after which she became a part of the Caledonian Steam Packet Company's fleet, and by which time other steamers were serving that part of Arran as well. It is partly due to the *Ivanhoe* and partly due to the C.S.P.Co. that the south of Arran was developed.

By 1892, for reasons beyond the scope of this book, the C.S.P.Co. and the Glasgow & South Western Railway were both running steamers to Arran, the route for them both being Ardrossan to Brodick, then on to other piers. A local dignitary — a sort of Victorian version of the redoubtable Evelyn Sillars of the present day — suggested that instead of both companies ploughing the same furrow in the Clyde it would be more sensible if one of the companies routed Ardrossan—Brodick—Whiting Bay, while the other went Ardrossan—Whiting Bay—Brodick. The number of passengers travelling from Whiting Bay and the south of the island had increased, partly owing to the efforts of the south Arran omnibus operators and hotels, and it

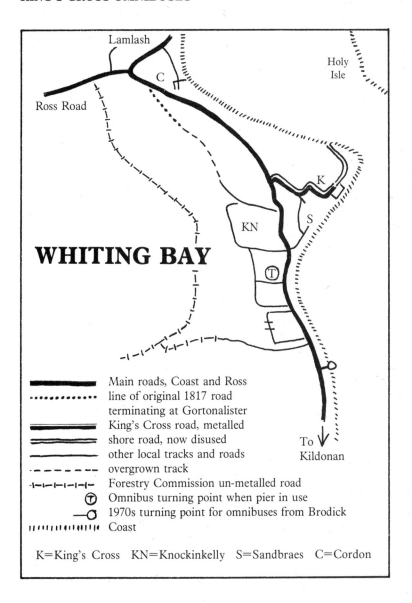

Lamlash

Holy
Isle

Ross Road

C

WHITING BAY

K

KN

S

T

To
Kildonan

▬▬▬▬▬	Main roads, Coast and Ross
••••••••••••	line of original 1817 road
	terminating at Gortonalister
▬▬▬▬▬	King's Cross road, metalled
▬▬▬▬▬	shore road, now disused
▬▬▬▬▬	other local tracks and roads
- - - - - -	overgrown track
-I-I-I-I-I-	Forestry Commission un-metalled road
Ⓣ	Omnibus turning point when pier in use
—O	1970s turning point for omnibuses from Brodick
ιιιιιιιιιιιιιιι	Coast

K=King's Cross KN=Knockinkelly S=Sandbraes C=Cordon

should be borne in mind that the quickest way to get from Whiting Bay to Lamlash or Brodick was by steamer.

The G.S.W.R. refused to initiate the new way round on the grounds that it had a mail contract, and certainly nobody could quarrel with the decision of the company if based on that reason. While declining to initiate such a routeing, the G.S.W. stated that it would not rule out the possibility of competing for Whiting Bay direct traffic if the Caledonian took that route. The Caledonian, after meetings with various interested parties in Whiting Bay, started the 'Whiting Bay first' run in early 1901, and it was an immediate success. The South Western started to retaliate after a six-week period of watching to see what happened, but the people from the south of Arran, aware that the 'Caley' had taken a chance, gave near total support to it, leaving the South Western with no option but to withdraw its own direct service and concentrate on the Brodick first sailings.

With excursions taken into account it could be that as many as eight steamers a day were calling at King's Cross by 1908 in summer months. To cope with them a consortium of local farmers, who had several rowing boats and a sailing boat for transfer to the steamers of their own produce, carried passengers to and from the steamers off the point for a charge (extra, and levied upon the passenger) of a penny, pre-decimal coinage. The nearest equivalent today is ½p but it should be borne in mind that an old penny in those days would take a passenger between two stations on the railways, and up to nine miles on a city tram. There was a road of sorts, which had been constructed and was maintained to accommodate carts travelling between the shore and the centre of King's Cross, which is a short way and a steep climb inland.

The transfer could be effected by just one boat as a rule. All three were about 24, or it may be 25 feet long. One had been used until 1901 at Whiting Bay, and is said to have been a 'sailing boat', although, in fact, it was rowed when used at all, with 'bare sticks'. In the height of summer two of the boats, and in extreme cases all three, would be required, but more often than not one of them was used for trips to Holy Isle or down to Lamlash — just one of the many attractions that Arran had to offer the visitors who were flocking to the island in ever-increasing numbers.

That, then, is the picture of King's Cross, a destination or an embarkation point for residents in and visitors to King's Cross, which covers a wide area, for Knockinkelly and for Sandbraes, and it remained so until 1924. Until then, John Cook had been responsible for the operation of the boats with assistance from such men as Neal Currie and Jim Cook. When John Cook died in 1923 the end was in sight. His son, Alistair, took over the responsibility, but in 1924 the London, Midland & Scottish Railway Co., formed the year before to merge and *rationalise* the activities of the 'Caley' and the 'Sou'western' deleted King's Cross from its timetable and, from that time on, by-passed it. This was partly due to the activities of the various operators of the King's Cross omnibus services, to which we will now return.

One of the earliest of these seems to have been James Hamilton, a resident of Knockinkelly. He had several carriages for hire, and although many of his journeys to King's Cross were to take steamer passengers in, or to bring disembarking passengers out, he was in the habit of uplifting passengers along the way when there was room for them. He also appears to have done well out of (and, of course, for) passengers who, after 1901, felt that the arrangements at Whiting Bay Pier were more suited to their own notions of the dignity incumbent upon them, or that the said arrangements were more conducive to safety — certainly he carried many people from Whiting Bay to King's Cross and from King's Cross to Whiting Bay, although whether on a taxi or an omnibus basis is, perhaps, open to argument. James Hamilton seems to have been at his most active from 1890 to 1905.

In King's Cross there lived one John MacKenzie, who had two very well-kept carriages, one of which — purchased new by him — was the first rubber-tyred vehicle in the island. He ran a regular omnibus type service from King's Cross to Whiting Bay, solely for people who preferred the pier embarkation and, in addition, he often advertised by word of mouth his intention to run an excursion to the Brodick Fair. Unfortunately, for him, there were a number of related MacKenzies in and around King's Cross who wanted to travel to Brodick Fair themselves, so John often found that an excursion trip for which he was, not unreasonably, expected to make some money, was nothing more than a MacKenzie family outing! Both of his carriages were very highly-polished mahogany — "and I should know," his son Ian once told me, "it was my job to polish them."

A.C. 'Pa' Lennox ran several horse-drawn carriages to and from

King's Cross regularly, and these were, for a time, eclipsed by the service offered by John Kerr.

He, Kerr, eventually obtained a GMC wagonette, SJ222 in 1918, and this ran not from Whiting Bay, but from Lamlash to King's Cross, and seems to have been the first King's Cross service for which there was some kind of timetable, although the unpublished times of the others I've mentioned were just as reliable. Kerr sold his GMC and several other motor cars to Ernest Bolt, who built a garage in Lamlash and operated there until 1935 when the whole business passed into the Lennox empire. Both Kerr and Bolt had operated the G.M.C. wagonette with an advantage that neither Hamilton nor MacKenzie had enjoyed — the withdrawal of the steamer connection at King's Cross point had led to the rapid deterioration of the road leading down to the shore, and this had necessitated the use of the Post Office forecourt as a terminal for the omnibus, thus saving a great deal of wear and tear on a primitive and under-powered vehicle on a fearsome and somewhat bumpy hill.

Older residents of King's Cross, some of whom now live in Montrose House, Brodick, have told me that Donald McLardy ran his motor car to and from Lamlash for King's Cross traffic in the early 1920s. This would have been SJ246, a dark blue Ford five–seater, registered to him in 1920.

Also said to have linked King's Cross and Whiting Bay with each other in those days were the two Chevrolets, SJ338 (1922) and SJ393 (1923) of Marion Sillars, and SJ345, Daniel Murray's Ford Tourer. These you may tend to regard as taxis rather than as omnibuses, although in fact a good many post–1930 (and, indeed, post–1960) omnibus departures have been operated by saloon cars, although this has been in the main confined to extensions which are scheduled as 'by request only' where the number of passengers travelling 'on' does not justify the use of a large omnibus.

Particularly when the omnibus driver would only have to bring the vehicle back to the garage, then retrace his route again, home in his own car to the place at which the 'extension by request' passengers were to be dropped off!

Duncan Kerr was another who had large hire cars which were often sent to King's Cross in the 1920s, although I gather that these often went 'on spec' and could be used from there to either Whiting Bay or back to Lamlash, from whence they had been sent in the first place. Duncan Kerr's cars seem to have done better than most, in that he often obtained a hire for an entire week to take a visiting family to various places in Arran for day trips.

There was a degree of competition between Lennox's and Gordon's on the King's Cross route between 1928 and 1932, after which they came to an agreement of co-operation as described elsewhere.

The regular service to King's Cross ceased in 1938.

At the present time there is a Scripture Union camping ground, owned, or at least permanently rented, by that organisation, and further down, at the bottom of the now all but overgrown road to the shore, there is a clearing in which the Boys' Brigade set up their tents in the summer. These two organisations, from time to time, block-book in advance by notifying the Arran Transport & Trading Company that they are coming, and the Ford minibus is used to carry them, partly to keep 20 bodies and rucksacks off an already busy service omnibus, and partly because the A.T.T. has some of the 'service to the public' tradition which has rubbed off on it.

That 'special' aside, however, there are now no omnibuses from the main A841 road to King's Cross, and all passengers from the only pier left in east Arran have to alight at the road-end and walk from there.

One day in the late summer of 1974 I was in conversation with a young woman who officiated as 'Conductress' on no less than three omnibuses on the Brodick to Whiting Bay route. If the steamer had disgorged more passengers than the one omnibus could physically (not necessarily legally) hold, then extra machines would be put on, and she would jump off one as soon as the fares were collected, then on to the third one as soon as she had taken the fares on the second. During our conversation I mentioned that she appeared to have lost her licence number plate, to which she replied: "I am too young to have a licence, but I've got the form, and I'll send it in the year after next."

McMILLAN, Pirnmill
Lochranza Pier—Catacol—
Lenimore—Pirnmill—Imachar

James McMillan was a butcher to trade, and later a grocer, in Pirnmill, in the days when meat and groceries came by steamers linking Glasgow with west Arran and Campbeltown. He had a horsedrawn van at first with which he used to uplift bulk consignments and deliver the 'messages'.

It seems that, like so many traders who had business at the pier, he found himself expected to uplift passengers for and from the steamer. It was possible to embark or disembark from the ship just off Pirnmill, a rowing boat ferrying passengers and goods to and from the steamer which hove to, but a spirit of adventure (bordering on the foolhardiness, from what I can gather) was necessary, so James McMillan carried people to and from the pier at Lochranza, from where it was possible to board the steamer in a more dignified manner. In addition, he would have had intending passengers from Lenimore and Catacol as well.

Shortly after he acquired a Ford motorvan he decided that a motor omnibus could be put to good use, although it was 1920 before it came on to the road. It was a Ford one–ton dual-purpose machine from Anderson of Pirnmill, with whom, by this time, McMillan was in competition for passenger traffic.

The Ford was used for passengers mainly, the lorry body was not used often. When there were no service runs to and from Lochranza the vehicle was used for tours. In addition to the competition for tours from Anderson there were several motor cars licensed for tours available at Lochranza. Alex. McMillan of Lochranza had SJ310, a brown Ford five–seater, registered in 1926, Ronald Neil McMillan had SJ290, a black Ford six–seater operating from the Lochranza Hotel, and James McBride who lived at Rose Cottage, Pirnmill, had a four-seat Ford SJ267 registered in 1921. Despite the 'same name' of some of these competitors they were not related — at any rate not closely.

The Ford omnibus was painted maroon, as was a later motor charabanc of which little is known. Although competition for private hires and tours between McMillan and Anderson was maintained, the omnibus service was the subject of an agreement in and after 1927 whereby the two Pirnmill-based competitors took it turn and turn on a day-on-day-off basis to provide the service car, with the operator whose turn it was not providing a relief omnibus to the requirement — if any — of the other one.

At the end of the 1929 season James Robertson sold his omnibus and motor business to Robertson of Blackwaterfoot, although it was not, as we shall see later, the last time that McMillan was to be the fleet name borne by west Arran omnibuses.

QUESTION: What is yellow and white and soft and goes round Arran in five hours?
ANSWER: Dan Stewart's sandwiches.

ANDERSON, Pirnmill
Lochranza Pier—Catacol—
Lenimore—Pirnmill—Imachar

Henry Ford, the motor manufacturer, once said that his customers could have a car any colour they liked, so long as the colour they liked was black. (He also said that "history is bunk" — I wonder how he would feel if he knew that he was to be mentioned in many history books?). He could also have said that Arran customers could buy a Ford car from any dealer in Arran, so long as that dealer was Anderson of Pirnmill.

Robert Anderson was a blacksmith in Pirnmill, well-established and highly thought of at the turn of the 19th–20th century. Like so many people who had business with horses, he had various horse-drawn conveyances for hire. The first of these was a gig, and by 1907 he had several vehicles, all horse-drawn of course, including a charabanc used for tours. (The destination board *ROUND ISLAND* is in my possession). Pirnmill was on a steamer route, and there were many visitors from the mainland, some just for the day, but most of them were in Pirnmill for a longer period.

The arrangements for joining the steamer at Pirnmill were rather awkward — a small stone-built waiting room was provided, although in practice most people waited in the tea-room which, with the Post Office and the smiddy, made up Robert Anderson's business. There would have been other people waiting as well for the mail which was ferried ashore by a small rowing boat which went out to the hove-to steamer, although many intending steamer passengers from as far south as Blackwaterfoot would have preferred to by-pass the ferry facility at Pirnmill, and at Machrie, in favour of the pier at Lochranza.

The idea of a regular omnibus does not seem to have occurred to

Robert Anderson until long after his neighbour, McMillan, started — although the first motor (as opposed to horse-drawn) omnibus ran for Anderson in competition with the horse-drawn conveyance of McMillan.

This came about, or started to come about, in 1913, when Johnny Anderson, the son of Robert, told his father that the business should be modernised, and that if it was not modernised he, Johnny, would go to Canada to join an uncle who was a blacksmith there. He also had uncles in Canada in the church and in agriculture. Fortunately for those of us who have lived in Pirnmill since 1913, Robert Anderson did modernise the business, and Johny stayed in Pirnmill. The modernisation took the form of purchasing not only a motor car, but obtaining the first car and lorry dealership in Arran, and Anderson's became a Ford dealer.

A T–type chassis (in later years a one–ton dual-purpose chassis), a sedan and a touring car were always kept in stock, together with many spares and accessories; and in addition, a bicycle and spares supply was established.

Robert and Johnny took it in turns to go to Manchester to pick up cars and dual-purpose chassis ordered by customers in Arran and in southern Argyllshire. There were several years between the original suggestion in 1913 and the implementation of the plan. The Great War intervened and Johnny went to France to assist with the maintenance and repair of the railway locomotives, cars and omnibuses pressed into service by the military. Among the vehicles he dealt with in France were the AEC 'B' type open-top double-deckers which were commandeered from the London General Omnibus Company, of which only B340 has been preserved. Johnny once told me that he considered a double-decker himself in later years but never got around to it.

(Unless otherwise stated, omnibus and coach numbers listed in this book are registration numbers. The number B340, however, is the fleet number allocated over and above the registration number to the vehicle by the LGOC. Arran's omnibus and coach operators did not apply fleet numbers to their vehicles.)

In 1919, he returned to Arran and the motor side of the business already mentioned took off. The omnibus he first used, built onto a one–ton Ford, of course was for tours only at first, but in time it was used for a regular run on an omnibus basis to and from Lochranza. It had a wagonette body and seated eight, but the competition it gave McMillan, the established omnibus operator, led to retaliation in the shape of the maroon Ford already mentioned in the chapter dealing with McMillan. This, in turn, led to the introduction of a white motor charabanc, a Berliet, a rather unusual vehicle for a Ford dealer to operate, one might think, and I cannot imagine how I never thought to ask Johnny about it before he died a few years ago at a very great age, but still hale and hearty.

The omnibus service was run on a regular basis throughout the 1920s, in competition with McMillan at first, with one driver asking the rival driver what fare was being charged that day, then under-cutting it, but by the middle of the decade a working agreement had been made, one of many in Arran, to take the road on a turn-and-turn-about basis.

Most of Johnny's 'empire' is still visible; the tea room and the shop have been split up and are under separate ownership, the garage/black-smith forge is still standing, and a little way up the burn will be seen the remains of the hydro-electric generator, the controls of which are in the garage. This equipment was installed and run for many years by Johnny Anderson, and is just one of the many improvements he made to the village he loved.

At the end of the 1929 season, with the Road Traffic Act looming, Johnny took the same view as many other small operators and sold his omnibuses and route to a larger operator, in this case Robertson of Blackwaterfoot.

**CLARK, Lochranza
Tours**

Lochranza in the late 1920s seems a strange place to which to return for work, particularly for a sea-going engineer in the middle of a depression. Many mariners returned home when their ships were laid up and there was no work, but those who came from remote and rural places were less inclined to do so. The rural and remote areas were usually concerned with fishing or farming, and neither of these industries had very much to offer to someone trained in the ways of a ship's engine room.

Donald McKinnon Clark, however, returned to his home village, and with a definite plan in mind. He had hopes of returning to the sea eventually, of course, but he was aware that the slump which had hit deep-sea shipping was not affecting the activities of passenger steamers on the Clyde, and that the passengers carried by the Clyde steamers were coming ashore for the afternoon in places like Lochranza in search of relaxation, scenery and charabanc trips. He decided to add one more vehicle to the number of those available, and just after he returned home he got started with a 14-seat Bean charabanc. It came to Donald Clark from the Grampian area, and was painted green with the legend 'Bonnie Glenshee' emblazoned on the back panel.

The tours proved to be very successful, the most popular being the Round Arran Tour, although half-tours of north Arran and the String road were also available, and these were often run twice a day, morning and afternoon. At odd times during the season Clark's charabanc would be hired by McMillan or Anderson, the Pirnmill operators, to provide extra seats on one of their tours, and by the same token Donald Clark would have chartered a machine from Pirnmill when demand was more than he could meet from his resources.

Donald's brother, John, had joined with him a few months after the start of the business, and he was instrumental in obtaining some motor cars. Donald took the view that the charabanc was sufficient but John thought otherwise, and proved to be right, for the Clark's motor cars and drivers were hired for day trips and picnic parties by families on holiday in Arran; a hire car had several advantages over a charabanc or bus trip in that a comparatively small party could stop when and where they chose, and for as long as they liked. Most of the hire cars were Buick — there was a Franklin Tourer as well. One of the Buick machines came to an abrupt end on the rocks at Catacol, when the mechanic who was testing it left the road on the way back to Lochranza.

In 1930 a Traffic Commissioners Court sat in Brodick to hear applications for and objections to licences for stage carriage and other services. Although Donald Clark presented a very good case for himself — he intended to run to the early steamer at Brodick — the fact that he had not done so went against him. This, together with the fact that there were already established omnibus operators on his proposed route gave the Commissioners no alternative but to refuse his application. A tour licence was granted but this was sold with 'Bonnie Glenshee' to Donald Robertson when Donald Clark returned to the sea in 1931.

Arran Coaches regret that their omnibuses are running five minutes late this week, but anticipate resuming normal service next week — when the omnibuses will again be running ten minutes late.

ROBERTSON, Blackwaterfoot
Lochranza—Catacol—Lenimore—
Pirnmill—Imachar—
Machrie—
Blackwaterfoot—Corriecravie—Lagg Hotel

Donald Robertson was born in 1903 and contracted poliomyelitis at the age of 18. After a struggle lasting many years, during which time he was an example of courage and tenacity, he managed a degree of mobility with the aid of a pair of crutches, and having established that he was not going to confine himself to a wheel chair, he cast about looking for something to do.

He purchased a Buick motor car from a family in Glasgow and engaged a driver with a view to operating a hire and taxi service. Within a short time he taught himself to drive and maintain the car himself, although, of course, the driver was kept on. It was at about this time that Clark of Lochranza and Anderson and McMillan at Pirnmill decided that they had come to the end of their own particular roads, so in 1930 Donald Robertson purchased the relevant parts of those three businesses and obtained a licence for an omnibus route from Lochranza to Blackwaterfoot, with extensions at certain times, to Lagg. Within a few weeks the demand was such that the Lagg extension became a part of the main route and all Robertson omnibuses went there.

With a line of route stretching from Lochranza through Blackwaterfoot Donald Robertson had a bit of schedule-juggling to do. His arrivals and departures at Lochranza would, naturally, be timed to coincide with the comings and goings of the steamers calling there. The steamer timings would also influence the timetables of Ribbeck and Newton omnibuses operating North Arran Motors, so all connections with steamers and with the 'end on junction' with omnibuses at Lochranza would dovetail. Omnibus connections with the services 'down the road' would have to be made as well. While the Machrie connection did not arise, since Weir's ran from Lochranza to Brodick via Machrie Moor, the connections at Blackwaterfoot with the Currie service, and at Lagg with those of Stewart's omnibuses which did not start from Blackwaterfoot, might well have been less easy to time, since both Currie's and Stewart's were running to and from the piers at Brodick, Lamlash and Whiting Bay, with their first priority being their own arrival times there. In such circumstances connections with Robertson would have come a long way second in their considerations, since even today the needs of internal passengers are fitted-in only after the requirements of those travelling to or from the pier.

By 1936 Robertsons was a sizeable organisation; the Harbour View Garage had been built, and housed several motor cars, and several omnibuses and coaches. The garage was known locally as 'The Jesters', and several explanations have been given for this. The first is that the building — a semi-prefabricated one — had been purchased from a travelling circus and had been the winter store for the clowns' equipment. The second explanation is that it was named after the drivers, some of whom are shown in the photograph section, who were noted for their humour. The 'Bonnie Glenshee' had gone by this time; a Dennis, new from the Guildford factory, and two Thorneycrofts from Basingstoke works were among the increased fleet. Some of the vehicles had the route painted on the sides, and others carried legends denoting their higher status as coaches-for-hire-and-tours. Aside from differences in the lettering on the sides, all passenger vehicles in the fleet were of a uniformly high standard of comfort, and painted mainly cream, with blue roof and stripes. Several lorries were at work in the island, with others based on the mainland (Argyllshire) and Robertsons had a contract to uplift milk from local farms for the Milk Marketing Board.

Local men, and some of Donald Robertson's relatives, were employed as omnibus drivers and conductors, as well as fitters. One of the conductors who was also a skilled panel-beater and fitter was Peter McMillan, son of the owner of one of the constituent parts of the Robertson route. The omnibus service was frequent, and several vehicles were required to maintain the one-hour each-way service which was operated during the summer. Winter services, of course, particularly north of Machrie and south of Blackwaterfoot, where there were overlapping services, were less frequent.

In 1947/48 the blue and white livery which was causing passengers a a good deal of confusion since it was similar to the colours of the Ribbeck omnibuses, newly-arrived in Blackwaterfoot, vice-Currie's, was changed to ivory, with black roof and stripe.

Donald Robertson died in 1952. The lorries were taken over by Bannatyne Motors and the responsibility for operating the omnibus and coach fleet was given to Peter McMillan, who took over the entire service later that year.

Robertson's

MOTOR SERVICE

To see Arran's Bens and Glens in Comfort, travel by our Luxury Coaches. We specialise in catering for all sizes of parties coming to the Island for a day Modern 20 and 29-Seater Sun Saloon Coaches and Private Cars -   -   - For Hire
Taxis to meet Commercials or Private Parties at Steamer
Schedule of Tours and Rates on Application
Telephone—Shiskine 229

Harbour View Garage

BLACKWATERFOOT • ARRAN

From an advertisement in the 1951 tour guide

McMILLAN, Blackwaterfoot
Lochranza—Catacol—Machrie—
Blackwaterfoot—Shiskine—
Brodick Pier—Brodick Castle

Peter McMillan, son of the operator of the Lochranza—Imachar route in the late 1920s, first appears on records of interest to readers of this book as the registered owner of SJ264, a blue Ford touring car, in 1921.

It is with his activities as an omnibus operator that we are concerned and these started at the death of Donald Robertson, for whom Peter had been working in several of the capacities that the 1940s and 1950s vintage 'busmen were all able to fill. He was a conductor, mechanic and panel beater, with some skill as a coach painter as well. Donald Robertson's death left his widow, now Mrs. W. Bannatyne of Brodick, with an omnibus and coach company which she was — in her own words — not too sure how to cope with, so Peter offered his services as manager. Within the year he made an offer to the owner for the entire business. When this was accepted Peter McMillan became the proprietor of a small fleet of Bedford and Commer coaches — the Thorneycrofts and the 'Bonnie Glenshee' (was it a Bean or a Halley?) had gone by then. As we have seen, the colours of the vehicles, which could still be described as 'new colours' were ivory and black.

Peter McMillan instituted one or two changes. The Blackwaterfoot garage was disposed of and the fleet was garaged on an individual basis, outside the houses of the various drivers, or behind Peter's Pirnmill residence, which had been the garage of his father's motor fleet. The Blackwaterfoot to Lagg extension was discontinued almost at once, this being 1952–53, when it was felt that the Stewart service between those two places was sufficient. Certain omnibuses were extended on to Shiskine from Blackwaterfoot, and the Northern terminal, Lochranza

Golf Course, was cut back to Lochranza Pier. With no scope for expansion — even if there had been a demand — the service was bounded by Ribbeck to the north, Weir to the west at Machrie (as well as competition from that firm between Lochranza and Machrie), with the newly-formed Bannatyne Motors to the west at Blackwaterfoot, and Stewart to the south, Peter McMillan ran a small service of omnibuses, with a few tours from time to time, and the whole thing just chugged away quietly until 1958, by which date it became clear that there was no need for two operators on the western side of north Arran, so most of the McMillan service was handed over to Weir of Machrie, after consultation with the Traffic Commissioners.

In addition to the omnibus service, Weir's took over the 'cinema' runs and what tours there were available were merged with those of Weir's. One McMillan vehicle and its driver — George Munro — were used for a Pirnmill to Lamlash via Machrie Moor and Brodick school run from Pirnmill at around 0800, returning from Lamlash at 1600. During the day the vehicle was kept at Ribbeck's and operated by them for and on behalf of McMillan on the Brodick Pier to Brodick Castle run which was then rather more frequent than it is now. This vehicle, and its route to the Castle, were handed over to Ribbeck in 1959, while Weir's took over the school run.

"Coaches, Sammy, is like guns — they requires to be loaded with very great care, afore they goes off." — Charles Dickens.

WEIR, Machrie
Lochranza—Catacol—Lenimore—
Pirnmill—Machrie—Blackwaterfoot—Lagg
Lenimore—Machrie—Brodick

Of all the buildings in Arran, the one which looks most as if it were purpose-built for public transport is that at the junction of the Machrie Moor and Coast roads at Machrie. The building — which reminded me of an Essex railway station the first time I saw it — has, in fact, been connected with passenger transport for more than a century, even to the extent of having a 'train' operating from it.

Despite restrictions of feuing and notwithstanding, indeed perhaps because of its remoteness and lack of facilities, the Machrie to Pirnmill area was noted as a popular resort as early as 1880, when a footpost was required every day in the summer months, reverting to just one day a week in the winter. The postman (known as a 'runner') was a very smart man named MacNicol; he had a beard, and polished riding boots, and usually made his deliveries on a pony. Unconfirmed reports (but from a source I've no reason to doubt) say that he used a trap during the summer, and although he did not regard it in any way as a passenger vehicle, it is likely that the class of person visiting the area and asking him for a lift along his route may well have given him a small (financial) token of their gratitude. (What a modern coach driver would call 'a drink' or 'a bung').

A sub-Post Office was established at Machrie in the spring of 1901, Mrs. Weir was appointed sub-postmistress and a part of the house was set aside as an office. It should be pointed out that the Weirs had for more than a decade prior to this been providing many of the services connected with horse-drawn transport of passengers and goods, though not on a regular basis, reliable though it was. Horse-drawn charabancs and other conveyances were available from Weirs well before the start of the 20th century, although the motor age appears to have come to them only after the Great War.

Weirs used interchangeable bodies on one of their early vehicles, and although interchange of goods and passenger bodies was by no means unusual on Ford chassis Charles M. Weir (the '& Sons' came later) had an Albion for this work, and that was rather less common. It could, I'm told, be shunted under a gantry, have the lorry body (complete with load of potatoes) lifted clear and a passenger body swung on, bolted down, and back on the road in less than 20 minutes. Never having seen it done, I am nevertheless willing to accept that this was not a universally-equalled achievement.

For an amusing title, it would be tempting to make a reference in the caption over the lorry photograph on Plate 41 to the effect that the wrong body was put on for a passenger run. Indeed, such a caption would, I know, give the Weir family much amusement, but the fact is that they were an extremely efficient organisation, and would never have done this. Further, I have had nothing but kindness and courtesy from all the Weirs with whom I have had dealings, and would not like to make fun of them — even in such an obviously affectionate way, so I must make it clear that the passengers in the Albion were going to pick some potatoes, that development of Mr. A. McKelvie whose Arran Pilot and Arran Banner potato first saw the light of day here.

Charles M. Weir had an early involvement with transport, certainly before 1880, after which date his horse-drawn lorries and passenger-carrying vehicles were a common sight on the roads linking Machrie with Lochranza and Brodick.

The first motor vehicles in the Weir fleet were Ford A and T-types, giving Weir a chance to tighten the omnibus service timetables which were, of course, compiled with the limitations of two or three horses in mind. In an area where Chevrolet, Bedford and Commer machines were the mainstay of all of the other fleets, Weir's were remarkable in that they tended more toward Albion products from Scotstoun; even their second-hand fleet had more of them than was usual in other parts of Arran.

The main business of the firm was transport of agricultural produce to the Ayrshire mainland and, of course, machinery and fertilizers, on the way back. Tours and private hires were in great demand, and a very high standard of finish was applied to all of the Private Hire and Coach Tour advertisements which, as one would expect of a small company, were hand-painted. The wooden boards with supplementary information, such as *PRIVATE, ON TOUR,* were white or yellow on black, with the lettering shaded with blues, reds and gold tinting which would not have disgraced the side of an SMT omnibus. A roller blind from a Weir coach, in my possession, shows such legends as *CORRIE, SANNOX, KILDONAN* and other places outwith the Weir line of routes which indicates that the firm was always prepared to re-hire its vehicles, and could do so without resorting to those crudely-painted boards that the A.T.T. finds acceptable for its own roller-blindless vehicles. *CHURCH* was also to be found on Weir's coach roller-blinds, and while *MACHRIE* would have done the job —and indeed, was on the screens, one cannot help but admire the style of a small undertaking in having, as it did, *GARAGE* as well.

Weir's had an advantage — of sorts; it depends upon how one looks at it — over other operators in that they had two separate routes serving (and tied to the times of) steamers arriving at and departing from two separate piers. The run from Lochranza which started and finished at the Golf Course was timed to meet the Campbeltown to Glasgow steamer at Lochranza Pier, after which it ran to Lagg. The other route to Brodick from Lenimore was, of course, running to and from a different steamer on the eastern coast at different times. This gave an extra domestic (or internal, if you prefer the term) service over the Lenimore/Thunderguy—Pirnmill—Whitefarland—Imachar—Dougarie—Machrie section common to both routes, thus giving a more evenly-spaced service up and down the north-west coast than other services elsewhere in Arran were able to provide.

The first diesel-engined vehicle — a lorry — to come to the island was brought here by Charles M. Weir and his brother, Duncan, and oil-engined omnibuses and coaches soon followed. One of the most notable was an extremely long (for its time) motor coach, an Albion, known locally as 'The Train', which was used almost entirely on the Lenimore—Machrie—Brodick run. The other noteworthy machine was the 1960 Scottish Motor Show Albion coach which was exhibited at Kelvin Hall, Glasgow, by the Albion company in 'Weir's Motor Services' colours before being delivered to Arran.

In the latter years a form of joint working with Robertsons was agreed on the Machrie to Lochranza section, and with Bannatyne Motors on the Machrie to Brodick section, whereby alternate runs would be made by the two competing services and, in the case of the Brodick section, the Weir omnibus running *not* over Machrie Moor, but to Blackwaterfoot, where an exchange was effected with Bannatyne Motors, who carried Weir passengers on to Brodick on one of their own scheduled departures. In later years, still omnibuses often went only as far as required; where nobody wanted to travel all the way through Lochranza, for instance, the last run of the day would terminate at the Pier, or even at Pirnmill or Machrie. At the same time (1958) the section between Blackwaterfoot and Lagg was discontinued, and the McMillan (ex-Robertson) competing service was absorbed into the Weir fleet. By this time, even though the private motor car was not so common as it had been for some years on the mainland, it nevertheless started to cause competition problems in north-west Arran, as was the case everywhere else on the island. A photograph I have seen shows passengers from the south or east being transferred from an omnibus into a motor car, and this became a regular feature of the Weir's Machrie to Lochranza section of route; sometimes not even sufficient passengers to fill a car, which in any case often needed to go only as far as Imachar.

Weir's Motor Services abandoned its omnibus and coach services in 1966 — and the word 'abandoned' is, alas, the best word to use. Certainly they tried as hard as they could — and harder than most — to keep a viable service going, use of private cars as 'feeders' to and from the withered arms of their routes where possible, introduction of special cheap day-returns, but, as many rural omnibus operators throughout Britain found in the early 1960s, it was the end of the Omnibus Age. In 1966 Weir's omnibuses and coaches were no more, the routes they had plied were served from then on by Bannatyne Motors, and Weir's were re-geared to service the private motor car — a service they still perform to the satisfaction of car owners as far away as Lamlash and Kilmory. In addition to car repairs, servicing, sales and spare parts, they also have a massive 6X6 ex-military (or it may be ex-Pickford's) wrecker truck which will pull anything in Arran out of anywhere in Arran. Truly, a magnificent beast!

Never having seen a Weir omnibus or coach — they were off the Arran roads seven years before I came here — I have had to rely on colour photographs made available to me by Mr. Duncan Weir; Mr. D. G. Weir, who is 'the boss' at Machrie now, the late, and very badly missed Mr. Grant Weir; and Mr. M. Morton Hunter. Some of these have been reproduced here in black and white but with all due deference to the other Arran omnibus operators who used the colours — Lennox, Arran Transport and the Scottish Postal Board — the red and white livery of Weir's Motor Service, as I see it, was the most striking of them all. Perhaps it was the shades of red and white, or perhaps it was the way the sun sinking in the western sky set-off the colours. Perhaps it was even the ink used to print the photographs. Whatever it was has now, like John Wayne at the end of the film, passed this way for the last time and into the sunset which, if you think about it, was just the opposite of what their major vehicle supplier had in mind.

'Sure as the sunrise' — *taken from a line in R.D.Blackmore's LORNA DOONE.*

BANNATYNE MOTORS, Blackwaterfoot
Blackwaterfoot—Kilpatrick—Corricravie—
Lagg—Kilmory—Low Kildonan—
Whiting Bay—Lamlash—Brodick
Brodick—String Road—Shiskine—Blackwaterfoot—
Machrie—Imachar—Pirnmill—
Lenimore—Catacol—Lochranza

On the 30th September, 1973 the last of the famous green omnibuses of the Bannatyne Motors fleet paused for a moment outside the Blackwaterfoot garage and the driver, Jim Bannatyne, stopped the engine while his wife took some photographs. This done, the engine re-started and the last of the Arran family-owned omnibuses drove into the garage. It was a Sunday, and 891ADV, the ex-Grey Cars/Devon General AEC Reliance had just returned from a Church Special. The green vehicles with their white roofs, red stripes and thistle badges did not change colour overnight, but all of them were now under the ownership of the Arran Transport & Trading Company Ltd., and those which were not disposed of on the mainland were soon repainted into the livery of the A.T.T. Co., *or scrapped.*

Even now, eight years on, as I write there are still traces of Bannatyne Motors omnibus operations; nobody walking in, or being driven through the south of Arran can fail to see one of the old coaches lying in a field or at the back of a farm, in use as a haystore or onion-drying shed.

Bannatyne Motors started operating omnibuses and coaches on 2nd April, 1952, when the Blackwaterfoot garage and String Road—Brodick omnibus service, started by Colin Currie, was purchased from Ribbeck's Motors, together with several omnibuses, by two Bannatyne cousins. There are more Bannatynes in Arran than you would care to shake a stick at, many of them have had some part in putting this history together — *and* with the research for this book. The two in question here are Donald E. Bannatyne and Donald S. Bannatyne, known throughout Arran then and now as 'Don' and 'Deeyess' respectively. Until the Spring of 1952 Don had occupied a small workshop at the rear of the Kinloch Hotel at Blackwaterfoot, in which he maintained and repaired motor cars. Deeyess was responsible for the operation of several lorries used, in the main, for carriage of farm produce and livestock, as well as other freight, from Arran to the Ayrshire mainland and beyond. The 'new' premises acquired from Ribbeck's became the base for both of these operations and the depot for the omnibus service as well.

The school contract whereby Bannatyne Motors carried children of secondary school age through to Arran High, the island's only secondary school, gave them a route which ran from Blackwaterfoot over the String Road to Brodick, then, subject to certain restrictions, on to Lamlash. The fare from Blackwaterfoot to Brodick 'over the String' was 22½p return, although in 1952 this was expressed in the pre-decimal coinage term – 4/6d.

In 1960 the services and three of the vehicles of Stewart, Corriecravie, were taken over and another vehicle was purchased, although the garage at Corriecravie was not required. Bannatyne Motors now had a complete circle of route right around the south of Arran and over the String Road. In addition to this certain omnibuses went up the west coast from Blackwaterfoot to Torbeg if requested.

Pocket timetables were issued in the middle 1960s; they folded six times to form a brochure measuring 7½" x 4¾" — and in reply to those people who have asked me what those measurements are in metric I can only say that Bannatyne Motors worked to feet and inches in those days. The brochures were well-designed and in addition to the timetable included a description of the parts of Arran through which the omnibuses were routed. When the brochure was folded a green base with black type took up the front cover and, when opened, a white base with black text and photographs did a tour guide which would not disgrace the Arran Official Guidebook. Wayside timetables were issued at the same time and these were on display in shop windows and on shop and cafe walls — there being no bus stops of a mainland type then or now in the island. The wayside timetables were on stiff card and measured 17" x 11". They gave a note on 'circular tickets' in addition to the times of omnibuses. These circular tickets were singles which allowed the passenger to get off any omnibus at any place, and get on to a later omnibus to complete the journey, and very handy, too, for people who wanted to see the standing stones or the Viking Fort on a circular (or part circular) trip in what Bannatyne Motors insisted on describing as 'green COACHES', although to be fair, their omnibuses *had* been coaches at one time, which is more than can be said for the successors to Bannatynes — but more of that at the appropriate time.

Bannatyne Motors, who always made it clear in their literature that their tickets were not interchangeable with those of any other company, took over the services of Weir, Machrie in 1966, and discontinued the Machrie—Machrie Moor—String Road end section of the Weir route to Brodick, which was incorporated into a Brodick—Blackwaterfoot—Machrie—Lochranza service, details of which were issued on a separate stiff card wayside timetable, without a map, and also incorporated into the folder.

There was a marked decline in traffic to and from Lochranza after 1971. As will be seen from the timetables for that year and for 1973, the early morning departure from Pirnmill to Lochranza and back to Blackwaterfoot was not required, since the steamers to and from Campbeltown had been withdrawn at the end of a previous summer. A ferry — of sorts — still links Lochranza with Argyll in the summer, but apart from a connection on the other side with a Postbus at 1200 for Tarbert, it is of little use to pedestrians, since there is no other public transport to or from Claonaig. So on 29th September, 1973 the Ford 16–seater Transit — the 'ice cream van' — left the Lochranza Pier at 1735 and Bannatyne Motors omnibuses never went back there.

The Bannatyne Motors omnibus and coach fleet was a motley collection; all of the passenger vehicles had seen a great deal of service elsewhere. Nevertheless, with coach seats, they were incredibly comfortable, and Don had — and still has — a genius for improvisation which ensured an almost total absence of 'down time' while defective parts were awaiting replacement. During the late 1960s several Albion coaches surplus to Bannatyne Motor's (and other operators') requirements, found their last resting places in farm yards, to which places Don often went with a screwdriver and spanner in search of a replacement steering wheel, gear lever — even a complete engine, I'm told, removed by Don almost single-handed from an inaccessible place high in the hills to which the 'donor' vehicle had been towed by a crawler tractor. There is a story — possibly apocryphal, although Don has never denied it — that an Albion ground to a halt on a Thursday morning apparently beyond economic repair. Nothing daunted, Don scanned the pages of *Exchange and Mart* and purchased a motor coach advertised in that magazine 'sight unseen', after which he thumbed a lift to England and drove it back to Arran, where it entered service early on the Saturday morning! Not to spoil a good tale, it is likely that 'thumbing a lift' took the form of travelling to England in one of his own lorries which was going that way, but the fact is, whatever way he went about it, Don Bannatyne was never beaten by a crisis.

The omnibus fleet included several Albions, including LAO160 which I assumed had come from Cumberland Motor Services Ltd., until their historian told me that it had not come from them but from Blue Band Motor Services. Several of the Albions had lightweight Scottish Aviation coachwork; there was a Maudslay with a Brockhouse body, a Foden (extremely rare machines but two came to Arran), and a Bedford with Duple coachwork, ex-Stewart's of Corriecravie. There was also the AEC already mentioned, and a 14–seat Karrier minibus which was replaced by the Ford Transit 16–seater now in the A.T.T. fleet.

Today, Bannatyne Motors concentrates on goods haulage, with regular runs to many parts of the mainland, and on car sales, car repair and maintenance and petrol sales. A small minibus is used to carry primary children to and from the school at Shiskine, and last time I saw Don he was just going out to sort out the problems of a customer who had locked his keys in his car. I've no doubt that Don took the problem in his stride.

PASSENGER: I say, conductor, do you stop at the Douglas Hotel?
DRIVER: No, hen, I can't afford it.

UP TO DATE

I am well aware that the events of the decade immediately preceding any particular date are not what is generally accepted as 'history', but what with mainland omnibuses which I still think of as 'new' being reported 'withdrawn from service and scrapped' in Ian Allan's *Buses* magazine, and all of the island police force looking younger than I do — where have the last 20 years gone, and why so quickly? I feel that in bringing this history up to date I am only deferring by a few weeks the time when somebody who is writing an Arran history will go to Montrose House (the Eventide Home at Brodick) to ask Bruce Hough's grandson: "When did they put the gas-turbine 400-seater onto the south-Arran run?"

In any case, when Maimie Smith gave me a *mint condition* 1892 Glasgow & South Western Railway timetable 75 years after it was printed, I started to think that perhaps the events of the late 1970s would be of interest to someone finding this book in the year 2070.

So look after it!

This look at the period 1973–1980 will be extremely parochial; although the Regional Council was supposed to have co-ordinated (and possibly even taken control of) public transport in the Strathclyde Region, it has not done so. Very few of the monthly issues of the *Buses* magazine (a national trade journal) have failed to criticise the shortcomings of the 'new' set up, and no sooner is one 'blunder' forgotten by the readers of Scottish daily newspapers than another one comes to light. The least-publicised effort at co-ordination was the printing of umpteen hundred 'Transclyde' stickers, which were stored in the Glasgow P.T.E. offices until (as one of its P.R.O.s told me) they could find someone in the organisation to persuade companies like A.T.T., West Coast, and A.A. Dodds, to put them on to their omnibuses operating in the area. As it happened, the 'Transclyde' stickers appeared in public on Corporation omnibuses and some British Railway trains, but in the two years since this happened 'they' are quietly changing the stickers to read 'Strathclyde'. At the end of 1981 Mr. Haddow at A.T.T. had not put any of these on to his omnibuses. Further, although tickets from Ardrossan South Beach Station can be issued (at the window or by ticket inspectors travelling on the trains) to anywhere on a railway line in Britain, it is not possible to book straight through from Neilston to Ardrossan, although both stations are in the co-ordinated, integrated Transclyde ('Links YOU Clydewide') system. It is necessary to book from Neilston to Glasgow, then queue at Glasgow and book again to Ardrossan.

I mention this only in case a 21st century historian, reading of the Transclyde co-ordinated transport scheme wants the point of view of a long-suffering and bewildered 20th century traveller; and to excuse myself to her or him for not discussing its impact in Arran. After eight or nine years of much-publicised existence, it is still a non-starter here.

Very little of what follows, then, was 'told to me' by retired coachmen or omnibus drivers' daughters. The last chapter closed with the last of the Bannatyne Motors service runs from Lochranza; it passed my window 48 hours after I came to live here. As my first love (what *was* her name?) used to say at the cinema, "This is where I came in".

There is no truth in the rumour that the Strathclyde Passenger Transport Executive Head Office is known as "The Circus" by virtue of the number of clowns who work there.

ARRAN TRANSPORT & TRADING COMPANY'S
'ARRAN COACHES'
— All Arran

The name Arran Transport & Trading Company first appeared just after the second German War, when Mr. Jimmie Latona used it as the title of his coastal shipping business. This consisted of two puffers, a type of small coastal vessel which was peculiar to, and much loved by inhabitants of the Clyde, West Highland seaboard, and Western Isles. They were the *Arran Rose* and the *Arran Monarch*, and although well-known in their day they are now gone, and only the name *Arran Rose* lingers on as the call sign of George Munro's car radio — which, incidentally, is at least 15 years older than the current CB craze. Although this book is not concerned with puffers, I heard a story concerning one of these two for which Neil Munro (no relation) would give his right hand, so we shall digress once more, this time into the world of Para Handy.

Arran Rose was not a lovely vessel; her funnel was out of proportion to the rest of her, and the engine room ventilators peered over the top of her wheelhouse like an old pair of riding boots leaning against a coach lantern. She was built as the *Stronshira* but by the time Jimmie Latona acquired her she was of uncertain temperament and her age was showing. Despite this she was put to good use, and Jimmie Latona got the best of her. As the years went by, she became more and more troublesome, and most of the fire brigades in the Clyde area got to know her quite well, as her engine room was constantly in need of pumping out, where, legend has it, the local fire brigade were adept at working round the engineer who was repairing a leaky seacock.

On one trip from Brodick to Troon she really came into her own — leaving Brodick at midday on Saturday she was fog-bound and suffering from a leaky boiler within an hour. The fires had to be drawn so that major repairs to the boiler could be effected by the engineer and it is a credit to him that she was able to steam again within six hours. Then the firebars gave way, depositing the coals into the ashpit, and once again was 'not under command for an hour or two'. In fact, it was eight o'clock the next morning before she got under way again. Visibility was still bad but the fog lifted in time to allow the skipper to note that he was approaching Ardrossan, at which point he turned to starboard and sailed to Troon, which place he reached at about tea-time on Sunday, having taken 30 hours.

Jimmie Latona's Arran Transport & Trading Company seems to have wound up in about 1953 and the *Arran Monarch*, which had been built in 1908 as the *Garmoyle*, went to the breaker's yard in Fife. As for *Arran Rose*, no firm word of her fate can be found — perhaps she is still steaming into a western harbour, with a fire brigade pump standing by.

To return to the present-day Arran Transport, a different outfit altogether, there are — or have been — one or two aspects of its operation which might seem to be as comic as those I've described; CJS888, for instance, a Bedford omnibus used on the Brodick to Catacol run, extended to Pirnmill after 1973. In addition to the plyboard side mentioned elsewhere, it will be remembered for its habit of boiling over at frequent intervals — I have seen it pulling off the road at Lochranza Golf Course on more than one occasion, surrounded by more steam than one would expect to see at a traction engine rally, and have assisted in filling its apparently bottomless radiator many times. Its driver, George Munro, took a pride in the vehicle, reflected in the care he showed nursing it over the hills, and I would not like to give the impression that I am poking fun — 888 was a good omnibus. In its day, that is, and its day was over long before it became part of the A.T.T. fleet. Since taking over responsibility for serving all of Arran's omnibus routes, however, the company has got rid of all of the older machines it inherited and at the time of writing has one of the most modern omnibus and coach fleets in Britain, small though it is.

Since taking over the last of the 'old' omnibus firms, the directors of Arran Transport (Robert Haddow, Margaret Haddow and David Warwick) have disposed of the Lamlash garage and relegated the ex-Lennox depot at Whiting Bay to the status of a store. Petrol sales, car sales and repairs, removals and haulage (a fleet of blue vans and lorries run to and from the mainland), sand extractions, a gift shop (now closed) and, of course, omnibus and coach operation are the main business of the company today, but it is only the omnibuses and coaches which are of interest here.

Mr. Jack Lennox is the omnibus operations manager — a thankless task to which he has become hardened. In common with most, if not all other omnibus companies, Arran Coaches comes in for a certain amount of criticism, much of it in its case coming from me in the form of semi-regular swipes through the columns of the local newspaper. Two days after one such 'swipe' I had to travel from Lamlash to Whiting Bay in an omnibus scheduled to return empty and out of service as soon as it got to the far end of Whiting Bay. I had to obtain one or two things from a Whiting Bay shop and wanted to go straight back. People who know Jack Lennox will not be surprised to learn that despite the fact that a service omnibus was only half an hour behind the 'empty-to-Brodick', Jack, who was driving the said empty vehicle, agreed to wait a few minutes for me, with that courtesy and good humour for which he is well-known. He made no reference to my recent article. Coals of fire!

As Shakespeare once nearly said, "— and some have lateness thrust upon them". The vessels used by the local steamer company on the Arran run, while suitable enough for carrying cars, are often delayed by bad weather. This gives A.T. & T. a big four-aspirin-and-do-not-slam-the-lid headache, for several reasons: (1) With the 'far ends' of its main routes being Pirnmill via Lochranza, Blackwaterfoot via south Arran and, in the summer time, Lochranza via Machrie, it is not possible for an omnibus leaving Brodick to be back for at least two hours: (2) See problem/reason 1.

Does the company hold the omnibuses against the late arrival of the steamer? If so, internal passengers waiting at, say, Lamlash for Kildonan, are kept waiting, without knowing why or for how long. Further, if the 1615 steamer is late, the omnibuses for west and north Arran are also carrying schoolchildren. If on time, the company can get the children home to Blackwaterfoot by about 1700 and to Pirnmill at about 1730. If not on time, irate telephone calls from understandably worried parents are the result.

Does the company forget about the steamer and roll the vehicles out on time? If so, passengers disembarking from a late-running steamer find that they have travelled perhaps 400 miles by omnibus, train and steamer to find that *as far as they can see* they have to take a taxi, or call a relative with a car because "the bus driver was so keen to get his tea that he would not wait a few minutes"!

Arran Coaches are rather like the old Highland Railway used to be. For most of the winter there is not sufficient full-time employment on an eight-hours-a-day basis for the machines or their drivers. Secondary schoolchildren are brought from all over the island, which means that there are omnibuses from all parts to Lamlash arriving just after nine; then there is not a great deal of passenger demand for the rest of the day until 4 p.m., when omnibuses once again leave Lamlash for all parts. There are internal services during the week, of course, but the winter months do not over-tax the capacity of the fleet.

Another winter problem, with schoolchildren and omnibus drivers living at the far ends of the routes is that a steady snow shower makes it necessary for all omnibuses parked for the day in Brodick or actually on a route, to get to Lamlash, uplift the children without waiting for school-closing time, and get them over the Glen Sannox road to Lochranza, over the String to the west, and round the south to Corriecravie before the snow makes the roads unsafe. Obviously, in such conditions winter schedules, such as they are, are disrupted.

Then comes the summer, with demand for omnibuses to and from the north, west and south linking all five steamer arrivals and departures; extra omnibuses between the pier and the Castle and between Brodick village and Whiting Bay (between steamer times) and coaches for Scotia, National, Barton, Wallace Arnold and other tours. This stretches men and machinery to near enough the breaking point but aside from two occasions when a service omnibus was taken off its scheduled run (the mid-afternoon Brodick—Lamlash—Whiting Bay) at five minutes' notice to operate an afternoon tour not arranged until a few minutes before, and aside from working to the winter timetable three days before the one in force was due to expire, the company has done as well as any organisation in keeping an omnibus service going in difficult circumstances.

Having said that it does very well when it comes to dealing with sudden emergencies beyond its control, I think it only fair to add that some of the crises are foreseeable — and what springs first to mind in this context is the practice of amending timetables (with ballpoint pen) as soon as they come from the printer. Another criticism here is that after years of comment from the public on the subject it rarely, if ever, gives an indication on the timetable that omnibus departures are 'subject to arrival of the steamer at Brodick' or that omnibuses scheduled to run to the south from Lamlash at 1600 leave from the school, which is to the south of where visitors wait, since they all assume that the omnibus will leave from the centre of the village.

That aside, statements in other books about modern-day Arran, like "......the bus service is almost non-existent" "...... bring your own car", or even "......if you don't mind a long wait for a bus" are not completely accurate, and do a great deal of harm to the tourist industry, since that type of statement is really applicable only to the winter. The 1968 Transport Act could have been of some benefit to the Arran omnibus services if only Bute County Council (as it then was) had used the powers conferred upon it to give a subsidy to the remaining companies, but this was not to be. Today Arran is governed by a District Council and a Regional Council, with the latter responsible for 'integration of public transport'. Since no two councillors or officials can agree what their terms of reference are in this matter, let alone agree a credible policy, it seems that A.T. & T. and other rural operators will come a long way behind in the list of priorities for public transport which, although they have been listed since before 1973, have not yet made any apparent impact outside Glasgow, aside from a few Transclyde stickers on some of the GCT omnibuses.

In addition to the summer and winter services detailed in Arran Coaches timetables, reproduced here, the company runs several tours, some of a week's duration, for the National Bus Company, Scotia Tours and others, and several day tours for other mainland companies who have sent their own 'Tour of Scotland' passengers for the day. The Round Arran Tour operated by Arran Coaches is designed to give individuals and small groups a tour of the island at an attractive rate. The 'Ten–A Tour', so called because it was once listed in the L.M.S.R. timetable as 'Tour 10A', waits at Brodick Pier from about ten minutes before the steamer is due, to about 15 minutes after it has arrived, thus allowing time for people to find how long they will be travelling for, where they will be stopping, and what time they are due back in

Brodick. It rolls out at around 1055 and goes to Lochranza via Corrie and Sannox, then round the coast road to Lagg, Kildonan High Road, Whiting Bay, Lamlash, and back to the pier at Brodick by 1615. It stops for refreshments several times, and as often as circumstances permit for the taking of photographs.

The company has tried several tours 'from the island' for Arran people. These have included trips to South Devon and to the Netherlands, and although they were a success in terms of the pleasure given to the patrons there was insufficient demand for the experiment to be repeated, although no doubt the company will make further experiments of this nature.

Two of the coaches travel to the mainland every Saturday in summer months; Danny Stewart to Carlisle, and Frank Hamilton to Sheffield, in 139 and 459 respectively, to uplift their passengers and bring them to the island for a week, during which time they are taken round Arran and over to Campbeltown by the same driver, and in the same coach, returning to the mainland the following Saturday. Also in summer months is the Scotia Tour, at present operated by 138 with Donny Campbell driving (to say nothing of joking, entertaining, and discharging the duties of driver, courier, guide, clown). As in the days of Lennox and Gordon, Arran coach drivers have their share of Christmas cards from people to whom they have played host the previous summer, and will play host to again the following season.

In 1976 the fleet consisted of: NSJ257N, NSJ258N, HCS350N, HCS351N, the standard service omnibuses, all identical, except that 350 and 351 have a Telma electric braking system. They are Bedford YRT type, with 45–seat Plaxton coachwork. All are fitted with Setright Key-speed ticket machines and were allocated —

257 — north Arran via Corrie; driver George Munro, Pirnmill
258 — south Arran; driver Neil Black, Whiting Bay
350 — north Arran via String; driver Donny Campbell, Blackwaterfoot
351 — south Arran; driver John Smith, King's Cross

AUP250B was a forward control Bedford SB41–seat Duple. Now gone.

SJ1340 is a normal control Bedford OB 29–seat Duple, stored.

3656WA a Bedford SB with Plaxton Embassy body. Now gone.

AJA898B a Bedford with Bella Vega body, now gone.

CSJ438L a Ford 16–seat minibus, ex Bannatyne. Used for Castle run.

Machines listed are basically red with white trim. Those listed below are white with red trim:

CRN947D, aside from its colour, identical to 898.

HVY783E Forward control Bedford/Plaxton used in 1976 by Danny Stewart for mainland-based tours. Lamlash.

CSJ400L Bedford YR/Plaxton Elite Express allocated to and labelled for Scotia Tours, driver Frank Hamilton. Brodick.

NSJ200M Bedford YRT/Plaxton Elite Express, the only 53–seater in the fleet, driven by Grant Weir, used for 10A tour.

The foregoing 1976 fleet list shows the villages in which the vehicles were kept overnight. In all cases except Brodick they were kept outside their drivers' houses.

Arran Coaches drivers in 1976 were: Grant Weir, Fergie Latona, Danny Stewart, Colin Cox, Frank Hamilton, George Munro, Donny Campbell, Neil Black, John Smith, John Busby, Ralston Green, Charlie Hendry, and Alastair MacBride.

Since then there have been some changes. Fergie Latona died after a short illness and Grant Weir died suddenly at the end of a Ten–A Tour. George Munro has retired, John Smith, John Busby and Neil Black have taken other work in the island. To cope with acute vehicle shortages in the 1978 and 1979 seasons, the company hired two coaches from the mainland; both have since been returned.

There have been experiments in previous years with a day trip to Glasgow using an A.T.T. vehicle from Brodick, over on the steamer to a parking place in Glasgow where the driver waits all day to take custody of the 'messages' obtained by the passengers who can then make further unencumbered forays into Glasgow shops. This experiment seems to have been accepted as successful by the company; this year it was due to be run on three separate Fridays in late November and early December.

Arran Coaches drivers in 1981 were Danny Stewart, Donny Campbell, Alastair MacBride, Bruce Hough, Alistair Nicholson, Kevin Kilshaw, Andy Lane, Phil Broomhead and Frank Hamilton.

The fleet list in 1981 is:

257, 258, 350, 351, 438, 783, 400, 200, and 1340 (stored)

PSD845R (used for Scotia, 1978–79) now on tours.

CCS459T used for Scotia Tours at present.

MCS138W & MCS139W used for National tours and driven by Danny Stewart and Frank Hamilton.

An impressive line-up and while the management of the company might care to note that there is a little more to the concept of 'tradition' than exhibiting photographs of bygone Arran omnibuses, it can be said that with this, one of the most up-to-date omnibus and coach fleets in Europe, it can cope with the packman and his pack.

During the late 1970s two coaches were re-hired from the mainland, at different times, to take up the slack left by the premature retirement (by ATT standards of the day) of one of the existing coaches. One of the "foreigners" was a very smart Bedford YRT with Plaxton Elite III coachwork, called-in to deal with the Scotia tour for the summer. It was in West Coast Motors colours, although I understand that it did not come direct from that company; possibly it was one of theirs taken in part-exchange by SMT in respect of one of their newer machines. The other was a smaller edition of the same vehicle, but with 45 as opposed to 53 seats, and painted two shades of blue with black trim. It is with the second vehicle, the blue one, that this story is concerned.

It seems that during one particularly busy period just after the arrival of the mid-morning steamer, the blue coach was sent to the Holiday Fellowship with a load of 'punters direct' and that the orders given to the driver in respect of his movements after that were vague. It was a day on which the unflappable Jack Lennox was away from the island for a day or two and another of the company officers was directing operations. Somehow a party of people, who had been led to believe that the officer concerned would put them onto the north-

Arran omnibus, were left standing on a pierhead from which all omnibuses had disappeared. It was at this point that the hero of this tale turned round, rather pleased, no doubt, at the way in which he had expedited the departure of the omnibuses to the point whereby they were only ten minutes later than would have been the case—*was* the case—on other days when they were left to get on with it unsupervised, to see that he had left one or two (17 to be precise) loose ends in the shape of passengers, all wearing that trusting but bewildered look they all wear when a bus official gives them more than the time of day.

George Washington would have looked them fearlessly in the eye and said 'I regret that I forgot all about you, but something will be done to put matters right.' Mind you, George Washington would not have been of any use at all on the buses! Our hero did what nine out of ten busmen (myself included) would have done, to wit, 'covered himself' and then said that something would be done to put matters right. Unfortunately, in so doing he also did what only three out of ten busmen would have done, and over-reached himself. It is not clear if he batted an eyelid or not; the driver from whom I got this tale, an upright, trustworthy and honest youngster, was not prepared to embellish his story with tasty but possibly out-of-order frills. What is clear is that he surveyed the stranded party with a beaming smile and said, 'Right, I shall deal with you now', then went into the office, smoked a cigarette and, when he judged that the blue coach would be on its way back from Lamlash, went out and said, 'I have re-hired a vehicle from a neighbouring company. It will be here in a few minutes, a blue coach which will pick you up if you wait here.'

Quite what happened after that, I do not know; probably something quite embarrassing, since the driver of the blue coach, for want of any instructions to the contrary, did not return to Brodick at all. He parked in Lamlash and went for a cup of tea.

In presenting the first All Arran omnibus timetable for the winter of 1973, the Arran Transport & Trading Company Ltd. stated on the said timetable that they "would do all they could to maintain the viability of the winter services". Obviously it could not run an omnibus from Lochranza to the first steamer departure of the day from Brodick, so it went on to say:

"We have arranged with Mr. D. McAllister to provide a connection

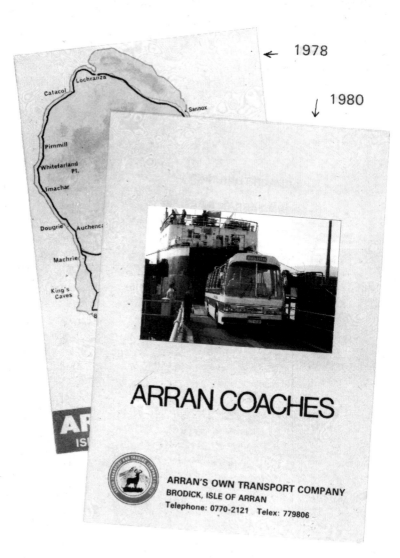

← 1978

↓ 1980

from Lochranza to Brodick for 8.20 a.m. (the steamer departure time) each day. Intending passengers should please telephone ..... for confirmation of times".

The late Duncan McAllister, J.P., left Lochranza every morning at 7 a.m. to travel to Brodick to meet the steamer, from which he uplifted the newspapers from the mainland for delivery to Brodick village and all shops round Arran (clockwise).

In the normal course of events he used a five–seat blue Toyota Estate car for this purpose and to fulfil the Lochranza to Pirnmill school scholar transport contract his wife used either a Bedford Dormobile 10–seater, or the other vehicle he owned, a 14–seat blue Ford Transit. The Transit was often lent to the late Reverend Jimmy Dow, minister of the churches at Pirnmill and Lochranza, so that he could uplift his parishioners on their way in to the church and take them home afterwards.

Despite the howls of protest which greeted the company's decision not to put a 'proper big bus' on to this departure, Duncan McAllister never had to use the larger vehicles; the Toyoto was always sufficient. Although the official route started at Lochranza, Duncan McAllister often went out of his way to uplift a passenger from Catacol (me) and on more than one occasion when it was not raining, and I had no reason not to walk in, but had overslept, he could be relied upon to go to Catacol to see where I had got to.

Duncan McAllister provided a service which was not, perhaps, unique in Britain, but it was nevertheless the smallest modern omnibus service in Arran.

Lamlash, Arran High School, Summer 1979. Omnibus arrived in from south, driver not had time to change the screen.
Passenger: "Are you going to Corrie? It says Brodick on the front."
Alistair Nicholson, driver: "It says India on the tyres, we aren't going there either."

POSTBUS, Brodick
Service 104 Brodick—Lamlash—Whiting Bay—
Kildonan—Shannnochie
Service 105 Brodick—Shiskine—Kilpatrick—
Blackwaterfoot—Torbeg—Machrie
Service 106 Brodick—Corrie—North Sannox—
Lochranza—Catacol—Pirnmill
Service 108 Brodick—Lamlash—Glenscorrodale—
Sliddery—Corriecravie—Kilmory

The numbers shown here are *not* route numbers exhibited on the front of the vehicles. Route numbers, as we know them, were invented by the Commissioner of Metropolitan Police (known in those days as 'Chief Constable'), a chap named Bassom. His idea was that instead of saying "the 'bus that goes from Hammersmith, through Kensington to Hyde Park Corner, then on to Piccadilly, then on to Aldgate by way of Cannon Street" it would be quicker to say '9'. To distinguish that route (9) from the one which leaves Hammersmith and also goes to some of the same places by a different route, the number '11' should be used. In this case, however, the numbers are used by the Post Office as reference and timetable numbers, nothing more.

Initial proposals for Postbuses in Arran were made in 1974, at a time when Arran Transport had only recently taken over responsibility for an all-Arran service. It was — naturally — reluctant to agree to anything that might affect the viability of a service it was trying to operate on what might fairly be described as a 'survival' basis.

"At a later stage, the Isle of Arran Council for Social Service took an active interest. They invited the Post Office to explain their scheme at a meeting of their Executive Committee. At a later meeting A.T. & T. accepted an invitation to speak about Postbuses as they affect their business operations. These two meetings produced an atmosphere conducive to Postbuses working as an adjunct to normal public transport and enabled the Post Office to proceed with the scheme which was eventually introduced.

"I feel that the Arran Council for Social Services are due a full measure of credit for their efforts on behalf of the Arran residents."

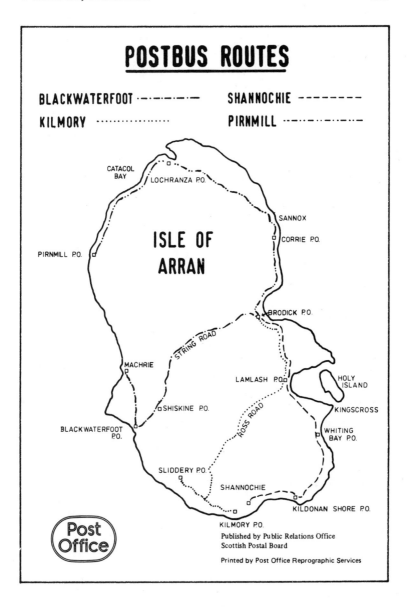

POSTBUS ROUTES

BLACKWATERFOOT —·—·—·— SHANNOCHIE — — — — —

KILMORY ············· PIRNMILL —··—··—··—

CATACOL BAY

LOCHRANZA P.O.

SANNOX

CORRIE P.O.

ISLE OF ARRAN

PIRNMILL P.O.

BRODICK P.O.

STRING ROAD

MACHRIE

LAMLASH P.O.

HOLY ISLAND

SHISKINE P.O.

ROSS ROAD

KINGSCROSS

BLACKWATERFOOT P.O.

WHITING BAY P.O.

SLIDDERY P.O.

SHANNOCHIE

KILDONAN SHORE P.O.

KILMORY P.O.

Post Office

Published by Public Relations Office
Scottish Postal Board

Printed by Post Office Reprographic Services

The foregoing paragraph is taken from a letter to me from Kilmarnock himself, Mr. D. F. Francey, the Assistant Head Postmaster, and I should like to underline the last three lines, since it is not often that any council in, or for, Arran can see beyond a 10p per head, 15-minute trip, 20-minute headway ferry service to the mainland, connected to a Brodick—Whiting Bay Motorway, such being their idea of 'transport'.

In the summer of 1977, several 'Posties' went to Kilmarnock to take the PSV driving test. I do not think that was absolutely necessary, since the vehicles they drive are four- and 11–seaters. On the other hand, it is an indication of the seriousness with which the Post Office — and its drivers — takes passenger safety. This led to a reshuffle of postmen and women. So far as Lamlash was concerned, our two Posties, Jean Lane and Sal Bannatyne retired, as did their relief, Ruth Young, and Andy Knox came off the Pirnmill run to 'do' Lamlash. By the end of 1978 the position was:

Brodick to	Reg. No.	Fleet No	Driver
Pirnmill	RSD355R	5750074	Neil Kerr
Shannochie	NSB493R	5750072	Louis Joss
Blackwaterfoot	RSD354R	5750105	Willie Southgate
Kilmory	KSA948P	5750016	Roy Dickie†
Spare	YRS627M	5750063	Geo. McKechnie

† Roy Dickie commenced the Kilmory run a year later, in 1978, and shortly after this the Blackwaterfoot run was amended to its present form.

Fleetnames carried on the vehicles read *Royal Mail Bus* (it has just struck me that Her Majesty Queen Elizabeth might well qualify to join the list of Arran's omnibus operators!). Fleetnumbers are carried over the windscreen on Land Rovers (016, 063 and 105). *Scottish Postal Board, Operations Div., Edinburgh* is carried on the lower nearside of all vehicles.

Land Rovers are used on Blackwaterfoot, Kilmory and 'spare' Commers (072 and 074) were used on Shannochie and Pirnmill respectively. Since the service started, there have been several changes, the most notable being the death of Willie Southgate. He was

In 1971 there was one postbus service in Scotland. Today there are over 120. They provide a basic public transport service over more than 2,500 miles of road, most of which, a few years ago, were without pasenger transport services of any kind. They cover 2 million miles a year carrying well over 160,000 passengers. They provide a small but useful supplement to Post Office revenue in areas where traditional postal services are inevitably uneconomic. They do all this at minimum cost to Government or local authority funds.

The first postbus was introduced into Scotland in 1968. It still runs between Dunbar and Innerwick in East Lothian, just 25 miles from Edinburgh. This was one of four experimental services (the others being in Wales, Devon and the Lake District) introduced by the Post Office in 1967/68.

The postbus is, first and foremost, a mail van with a postal job to do. The needs of the postal service are paramount and although there is a certain measure of flexibility which can be deployed for the benefit of the bus passenger through the retiming of postal deliveries, this is limited and can usually be done only with the full consent of the people served by the postbus route. The combination of a passenger with a postal delivery service inevitably makes that particular run slow giving the passengers the opportunity to enjoy some splendid scenery. On the other hand collection runs are much faster and usually much more direct.

The typical postbus gives a twice daily service on the main route over which it runs. The first morning (sometimes early morning) service will be the delivery run, perhaps taking two hours or more to cover a 15 mile run. The bus will then return to base, stopping only to set down or pick up passengers. There will follow an afternoon run, this time giving a fast run out to the distant end, stopping on the return journey only for passengers and to collect mail from post offices and wayside post boxes. Only a few buses, however, conform strictly to this basic pattern. Some in very remote areas, where collections are made at the same time as deliveries, run once a day only. Others, where mail vans have to be sent, for example, to ferry terminals or airports to collect incoming mail, may run more frequently. In some places the postbus is used for carrying children to and from school. Each route has to be surveyed separately to ensure that maximum benefit is obtained from the passenger operation without impairing in an unacceptable way the postal operation.

The essential feature of the postbus service is that it should be efficient and cheap. Postbuses are therefore acquired to do the job they have to do and no more. There are no frills. So far, the basic vehicle has been an 11-seater Commer minibus which can be obtained to PSV specifications and requires minimum adaptation. In some parts of Scotland, however, a Commer was not suitable because of the terrain over which the bus had to pass. In these areas we already use Land Rovers for postal deliveries and since these are generally among the most sparsely populated areas, we asked for and obtained permits to operate bus services using 4-seater Land Rovers. This led to an examination of other very remote areas where a Commer was excessively big but where the terrain did not call for a general purpose vehicle. In these areas we are now operating bus services using Morris Marina and Chrysler Avenger estate cars. In one case, Laide to Achnasheen in Wester Ross, we are using a bigger vehicle, Ford Transit, and there are a few other routes where we have to use midi-, rather than mini-buses. These are very few and we expect the typical postbus of the future to be not very different from the 11-seater Commer.

SCOTTISH POSTAL BOARD
West Port House
102 West Port, Edinburgh EH3 9HS

POSTBUS LITERATURE, 1979

replaced by Ron Murray on the Blackwaterfoot run. George McKechnie, although he has a PSV licence, does the Whiting Bay non-passenger local round, and the spare driver is now Neil Kerr, whose Pirnmill run has been taken over by Danny Craig. On the subject of 'spares' there have been times when a PSV-registered vehicle has broken down and been replaced temporarily by a non-PSV Land Rover. At such times passengers are still uplifted, but no fare is charged. The 'spare' man, that is to say the relief postie, used to be 'Boyda' Milton, who has now retired. His place was taken by Alice Lennox. At the time of writing both Louis Joss and Roy Dickie are off sick. Stewart Black (who has a PSV licence) is doing the Shannochie run, and Alice (who does not have one) is doing the Kilmory trip. She picks up passengers but, in line with Post Office policy, does not charge them. I must say that the Post Office policy of carrying passengers free when spare vehicles or staff are used is the very epitomy of 'service'.

New Land Rovers have replaced the old ones since the service started, and the Commer 11-seaters have been replaced with 11-seat Dodge machines, which are the same thing really.

My view is that the Post Office would do well to replace the Kilmory and the Shannochie vehicles with 11-seat long wheelbase Land Rovers. The Kilmory route, which passes through some of the finest scenery in Arran (on the Ross Road) is not seen at its best through the front or back windscreens of a four-seat Land Rover with no side windows, and the route could be promoted as a scenic route, and could carry more passengers if this was done. The Dodge, like the Commer, is a very fine vehicle, but I am sure that Chrysler will agree that it was not designed to negotiate some of the rough tracks it has to use, and even though Louis Joss drives with great care and extremely slowly on these stretches, the machine takes a great deal of 'stick'.

There are picking-up and setting-down restrictions applied to the Post Office between Brodick and Whiting Bay, although these apply only at times and on days when there is a company omnibus due. With extra schedules operated in summer months by A.T.T., the Postbuses do not show much in the way of profit from passengers, although it is the function of these vehicles to carry passengers in the winter when the A.T.T. is not so active. Winter or summer, there is no finer way of seeing, not just Arran's tarmacadam roads, but its byways as well, and

a return trip from Brodick (or elsewhere) to any one of the four
Postbus destinations cannot be recommended too highly.

Back in 1973 I can remember boarding a Bannatyne Motors
omnibus in Kilmory and changing to an A.T.T. bus at Lamlash to go to
Brodick at times when the High School closed for the day. Now, with
all public transport (at school closing time) run by Arran Transport, it
is possible to book right through. On certain days passengers from
south of Lamlash who are travelling to Brodick may have to change at
the High School, since the omnibus from the south sometimes goes
only as far as Lamlash before returning to the south at 1600.

It should also be noted that omnibuses shown in the A.T.T.
timetable as departing from Lamlash (not Brodick) for the south at
1600 leave from the school, not from the village. Despite the fact that
many visitors reading the timetable wait opposite the Post Office, and
in consequence miss an omnibus to the south, the company does not
seem to have realised the value to all concerned of a note in the
timetable to the effect that the school is the departure point.

Postbuses run through Lamlash for the south at around 0920. The
Brodick—Lamlash—Whiting Bay—Kildonan—Shannochie Postbus
turns down Bungalow Road to the left, then right on to the Shore
Road, stopping to deliver mail at the Council Offices — the only
delivery made by this vehicle in Lamlash. From there it runs on to the
main road again, and on to Whiting Bay. On its way back it stops at the
Lamlash Post Office, which is set back behind The Ship House then
runs direct, and not via Bungalow Road, to Brodick.

Right behind it (both ways) is another Postbus which runs from
Brodick direct to Lamlash Post Office. From there it runs along Mill
Road and on to a rough track (both shown by arrows) until it turns on
to the Ross Road, having by-passed half of Lamlash. On its way back it
runs from the Ross Road directly on to the Whiting Bay—Lamlash
road, then along past the council offices to a pillar box on the shore
road. From here it returns to Bungalow Road, up which it runs to the
Brodick road, then to Brodick Pier and Post Office from there.

Post and company omnibuses stop anywhere along the routes they
take, so long as they have room for more passengers, and so long as it is

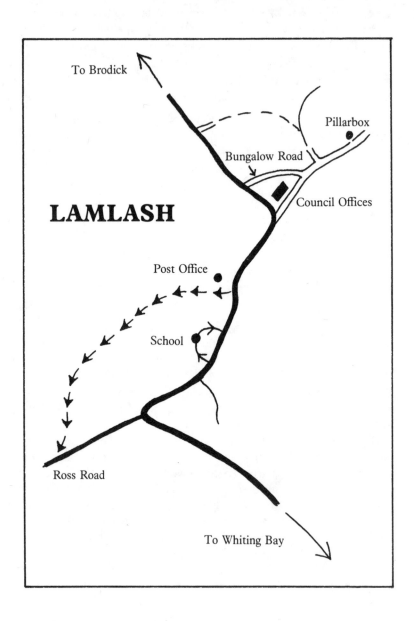

To Brodick

Pillarbox

Bungalow Road

LAMLASH

Council Offices

Post Office

School

Ross Road

To Whiting Bay

POSTBUS, BRODICK 171

safe to stop. There are no bus stops on the island but the villages have
regular stopping places at which most people wait.

Please give a clear signal in plenty of time to the driver of any
omnibus you wish to board. Just face the omnibus and raise your hand.
Hill tops and sharp bends in the road are not a good place to wait for an
omnibus.

One of the most popular places in Arran, so far as the visitor to the
island is concerned, is Brodick Castle, and for the benefit of any reader
who may wish to visit that place by omnibus I have included a sketch
map showing the routes followed.

The thick lines on the map on page 172 indicate the main roads
which serve Brodick.

The Brodick Pier—Brodick Castle omnibus service runs from the
pier, along through the village, past the Heritage Museum and on to
the Nature Centre. From here the Corrie road is followed as far as the
North Gate into which omnibuses turn on to the Castle road as a
broken line. After setting-down and picking-up the omnibuses then
continue southward along the Castle Road (which is a private road not
designated as a public highway) until they reach the main road at the
South gate, adjacent to the String Road-end. From here they return to
the pier via the Heritage Museum and the village. The section String
Road—Nature Centre—Castle—String Road is one-way only, anti-
clockwise, with the section Brodick Pier—Village—Museum—String
Road being two-way.

The North Arran (via Corrie) Postbus leaves Brodick Post Office
just after 0910 and runs via the school—Museum—String Road-end,
then turns into the Castle road and runs on through the Castle
grounds and out on to the Corrie Road at the North Gate. It does not
make its north-bound run along the main road past the Nature Centre.
On its way back it runs direct to Brodick from Corrie, via the Nature
Centre, and does not route through the Castle grounds. Unlike the
Arran Coaches omnibus which, as we've seen, runs through to the
pier, the Postbus ends its route opposite the Post Office.

In addition to these two services there is the North Arran Brodick—
Corrie—Sannox—Lochranza route of Arran Coaches, which runs in
both directions along the main road, stopping at the Nature Centre,
right opposite a gate leading (pedestrians only) to the Castle. This stop,

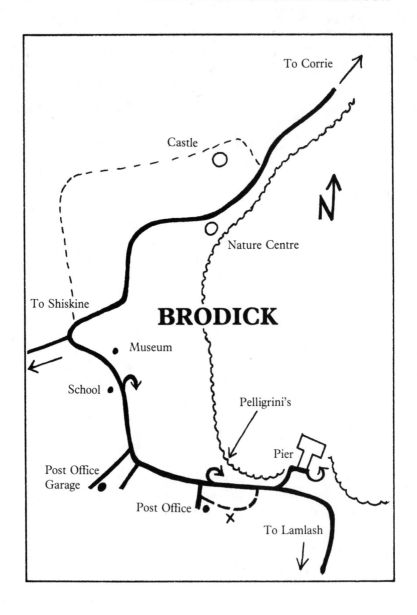

To Corrie

Castle

Nature Centre

N

To Shiskine

BRODICK

Museum

School

Pelligrini's

Pier

Post Office
Garage

Post Office

To Lamlash

incidentally, is equally handy for the Nature Centre and its cafe. All omnibuses from the north (Post and A.T.T.) stop at the Nature Centre on the way back to Brodick and are usually timed to add to (not duplicate) departures from the Castle.

During the period covered by this book there have been several terminal points in Brodick village, although all passenger-carrying vehicles have eventually arrived at Brodick Pier since it was built in 1872.

All omnibuses *except Postbuses* from the north or west — Lochranza, Sannox and Corrie or Pirnmill, Blackwaterfoot and Shiskine run through the village and terminate at Brodick Pier and, in addition, omnibuses on the Brodick Castle Service start from and terminate at the Pier.

In years gone by omnibuses from the south via Lamlash turned at various places in the village, opposite the Golf Club's 19th hole by reversing into the road marked 'T', or by reversing into the road by the Post Office (see page 172).

Today, unless circumstances (traffic, refuelling) dictate, some omnibuses by-pass the Pier on their way from Lamlash and turn at Pelligrini's shop, with a small lane between the shop and the Royal Bank of Scotland. Until very recently it was necessary for omnibuses to reverse into the lane but now an extended lay-by opposite gives sufficient room to turn in a tight circle. Unfortunately there are the same number of letters and spaces in the legend *Bus Only* as in the legend *Car Park*, and motorists tend to confuse the two, which, not surprisingly, discourages omnibus drivers from the south running down to Pelligrini's. Since they cannot see round the bend they tend to turn in to the pier without 'chancing it' and I, for one, do not blame them, since it is not very amusing to tell passengers for the steamer to remain in their seats until the omnibus returns to the pier, and then find that they have to spend five minutes — and take risks — to turn round.

One omnibus on the mass departure from Lamlash, Arran High School, by-passes the pier altogether at 1610 and continues on to Brodick Primary School, dropping-off High School scholars on the way, after which it turns in a layby/road-end opposite the school and returns out of service to the pier. An omnibus runs to and from the point X on the Alma Terrace, shown on the map on page 172 in broken lines, for schoolchildren attending Brodick Primary School.

Postbuses from the north and west terminate opposite the Post Office.

Brodick Pier, Summer 1982. Punters off the steamer wanting the Castle are directed to the Ford minibus by Jack Lennox. One of them sits behind the wheel!

Brodick Pier, Summer 1982. Driver Phil Broomhead comes in with No.351 and is reallocated to No.257. Full load of passengers, rear seat cushions on No.257 missing. Driver "liberates" back seat cushions from No.351 and takes them to No.257. Passenger: "Look at that, they are putting extra seats in!"

BUS SHELTERS

One of the more bizarre examples of the English idiom, I've always thought, at least since a Frenchwoman of my acquaintance once asked me:

"What zat funnee thing is there pliss?"

She was rather surprised when I told her that it was a bus shelter; it seems that in her country they are usually much larger and are known as 'depots' or 'garages'.

There are several categories of what might be described as bus shelters in Arran; the wooden and stone-built structures which, while built alongside or near to a road, have their 'open front' facing in such a way that the omnibuses serving that side of the road tend to sneak past without the shelter occupants seeing them until it is too late although, to be fair, the omnibus drivers in general (and Andy Lane in particular) try their best to slow down and pick up intending passengers who have not heard the omnibus coming. Of these shelters the most remarkable is the one at Glen Ashdale, at the south end of Whiting Bay. This was painted a few years ago by Arran Community Arts — the result is shown on Plate 108, and to those (particularly council officials) who say that it is out of keeping/character/ order (delete — or dilute — to taste!) I can only reply that it is much better than most of the others which, in the absence of either community art or — and more to the point — council attention, have had to make do with the attentions of a Mr. Kilroy.

A wooden shelter with perspex windows which, unlike those mentioned, was sited with passengers (as opposed to walkers) in mind, was put up at the junction of the Corriegills and Brodick to Lamlash roads. Not the safest place to put a bus shelter but it keeps the rain off the schoolchildren. Shortly after it was erected, at the insistence of the local District Councillor, Mrs. Evelyn Sillars, M.A., J.P., M.B.E., a cartoon appeared in the local newspaper depicting two people waiting in it. "All we need now", said one, "are some buses".

The other shelters which were built and sited as bus shelters came in 1980. One of them was erected opposite the Whiting Bay Primary School after pressure from the local Regional Councillor, Mr. Richard Wilkinson. I do not know how much thanks the two councillors got from parents of the schoolchildren concerned, but the '1980 perspex in frame on slabs' shelters were also the subject of a photo-cartoon. It was printed in the *Arran Banana*, a one-off magazine produced by Marc Head, the retiring editor of *The Arran Banner*.

I should not like any 21st century reader to imagine that I am attempting to make fun of the efforts of the two councillors in respect of the bus shelters. The 'Sillars' shelter at Corriegills Road-end has kept the rain off me many times, and the 'Wilkinson' shelter is where I wait — unaccompanied in my case — each day for an omnibus.

Winter, 1981, Lamlash. Pouring with rain. Andy Lane takes his omnibus out of its park, runs "back the way" and double shunts so as to uplift all the passengers who are getting wet waiting for the service car ten minutes behind, before running light to Brodick.

AND FINALLY . . . . .

On Monday, 22nd February, 1982 a delegation of five members of Parliament were coming to Arran, on behalf of the House of Commons Standing Committee on Scottish Affairs. With them would be some House of Commons officials and Strathclyde Regional Council officials. They were coming to inspect some aspects of the local transport as part of an overall enquiry into ferries and rural transport, to suggest ways to Parliament in which it might be made more effective, and ways in which funding might be improved.

Although this visitation was obviously not being made for the same reasons as the investigation mentioned in the chapter dealing with the projected light railway suggested in the 1919 Report, I thought that even though this book will probably be published before the report it might be interesting to see what this delegation did, since the way it would be going about it would not be too different from the way its predecessors set about compiling the 1919 document. Accordingly, I met the delegation off the steamer, and asked the Chairman, Mr. David Lambie, the South Ayrshire M.P., if I could be included in the party, and, of course, told him why I wanted to come. He took my request without batting an eyelid and said that I should be most welcome.

Although rural omnibus services were part of its brief, the party was understandably more concerned with the steamer services to and from the island, and spent some time watching the interchange of passengers between the steamer and the omnibuses waiting on the pier, after which it went to examine the vehicle loading ramp and its approach road. This done, it went into the offices of the Arran Transport & Trading Company Limited for a discussion, and to hear the 'company'

point of view of local omnibuses and of the lorries it sends to and from
the mainland. Sandy Gauld, the Brodick Postmaster; the island's
resident District Councillor, Mrs. Evelyn Sillars, and the island's
mainland resident (but on the island more often than not) Regional
Councillor Wilkinson, joined the delegation, and we all piled into
PSD 845R to be driven clockwise round the island by Alastair
MacBride of 'spider' fame.

On the way round the island the Regional and District officials
spent most of their time looking at maps and examining the roads — all
of those chaps are in the island often, of course; and while Evelyn
Sillars was talking to David Lambie, Richard Wilkinson was in
conversation with the local M.P. (Bute & North Ayrshire) John
Corrie. What they were talking about I do not know but since the two
councillors never miss a chance to air Arran's problems, and since the
two M.P.s were clearly not just along for a joy ride, I'm sure that
something will eventually come out of it all.

While the coach was passing Lavencorrach (a small cluster of
houses perched on a hill above the road, and connected to it by a
muddy, steep track) the Postmaster was able to show the delegation
one of his Postbuses in action. It was the Shannochie route 11–seat
Dodge, driven by Stuart Black — Louis Joss, the regular driver, was off
sick — and very impressive it looked too, perched high on the top of a
climb that Hannibal would have chickened out of, elephants and all.

On arrival at Blackwaterfoot there was a lunch-and-discussion stop
in the Kinloch Hotel, where photographs of old Col Currie adorn the
walls, and members of various local organisations met the delegation
to discuss the transport problems as they saw them. The organisations
represented included the National Farmer's Union and Bannatyne
Motors who were — understandably — more concerned with freight
charges and the cost of sending lorries to and from the mainland.
Passengers' problems were raised by the Council for Social Service
and the Tourist Organisation, although since no trace of any request
for 'evidence' from internal omnibus passengers can be found in any
local newspaper during the preceding month it is not surprising that
most of the problems raised at this meeting were in respect of steamer,
and not omnibus passengers.

At 1420 the delegation got back into the coach — the driver

demonstrated his spider on the way past the King's Cave turn-off — and the whole shooting match shifted its ground to Lochranza, where a stop was made to inspect the slipway and pier there, after which the coach took everyone back to Brodick. Coincidentally, a major problem was observed at first-hand on the way through Corrie; a Regional Council Road gang, with its lorry, was patching a hole in the road on the south side of the harbour, and Arran roads being what they are, we, and all other traffic, were obliged to wait for five minutes. This is a problem that can never be overcome, since with cliffs on one side, and the sea on the other, an improvement to the road can be made only at the expense of the village itself, and clearly, that is a piece of vandalism of which nobody — M.P., councillor, official or resident — would think.

The delegation was also to consider evidence in Islay, the Borders and Aberdeen. With an all-party committee considering the findings and suggestions, the eventual report may well be a compromise. As to the improvements — and they will certainly come — a 21st century historian will have to deal with them.

I hope this book, and this last chapter in particular, will be a base from which to start. The first 150 years of public transport in Arran at which we have been looking are now ended, and the omnibuses of today's Arran are subsidised and watched over to a greater extent than the District and Regional Councils are given credit for. It would be fair, I think, to stress this, since they do receive a great deal of criticism.

Even so, I bet they still won't give us a light railway!

And so we come to the end of a story of 150 years of public transport in the Isle of Arran.

If we have derived some amusement from some of the activities of the early pioneers and modern-day operators it is — for me, at any rate — affectionate amusement, with a touch of amazement and a great deal of respect. A transport writer once said of a small independent railway company that it had "struggled against adversity and over mountains, to arrive at a moderate usefulness". In applying that statement to Arran's 1980s omnibus, coaching and Postbus services, I do not intend it to be the deliberate sneer intended for the railway company thus described. They have, indeed, struggled over mountains, and have been no stranger to adversity. As to 'moderate' usefulness, I can only draw to your attention the chap who prodded the existing company into providing a very early omnibus for the first steamer departure of the day, then passed that omnibus, going in the same direction, in his own private car! Arran's public transport services cannot be run as an empty 'back-up' system for the rare use of motor car users who have a breakdown, or for some other reason only to look for an omnibus once every two years and wonder why it is not there.

During the next 150 years petrol, diesel and other such fuels will be exhausted, and the age of the motor car will be over. Car users will then ask about times of omnibuses to be told that the last one went 60 years ago because nobody ever used it. After a decade or so of walking it may be that someone will purchase a horse and invent a carriage to which to harness it. Possibly he will obtain a mail-carrying contract, and — could it be that he will make it known that he will be travelling to the pier at a certain time, that he will be following a set route — could it be that he will make known the sum of money expected from anyone who wants to ride with him?

> *There are plenty cars and 'buses*
> *To meet you at the pier,*
> *When once you've been I know you will*
> *Come back another year*
>
> *Now to this letter don't reply,*
> *But come yourself and see,*
> *On Brodick folk you can rely*
> *To be both frank and free!*

George MacGregor 1934

APPENDIX 1   **TICKETS**

There is a story that in the days before tickets were issued to fare-paying passengers and 'official' and 'staff' passes had been introduced, Thomas Tilling boarded one of his own omnibuses at a time when 'skimming' (keeping of a percentage of the takings) was considered to be the privilege of every omnibus conductor.

"Remember, my man," said Tilling as he handed the conductor his fare, "half of that money is mine!"

The first omnibus company to issue tickets in Arran was Ribbeck's — just one of the many 'firsts' to the credit of that family. They were introduced at the turn of the 19th/20th century and appeared at first as 'reservations' for the Corrie mail car made by passengers the day before. They took the form of a stiff orange-red card approximately 3½" by 2" in size, printed in black with the legend *CORRIE MAIL CAR RESERVATION*. Some of them, for the same period, said *CORRIE MAIL COACH* and the interesting thing here is that the 'Corrie' mail coach had been travelling on to Lochranza for some years. By 1905 the tickets were in the form of a slightly lighter card in the same colours with the legend *RIBBECK'S COACH TO...... 190..* They were issued to passengers for both omnibus runs and tours up to and including the Great War, at which time Col Currie was still finding one reason or another to speak to the driver — a method of assessing the number of passengers that he presumably felt to be more accurate than counting the number of tickets left.

As the motor omnibus age began to spread to Arran, the different companies had their own ideas of how their tickets should look, but all seemed to have the same idea when it came to printing them and for the period 1925–1960 — and even to the present day in some cases — the Glasgow Numerical Printing Company (GNP) were responsible for the provision of most tickets to Arran omnibus services. Examples of these are to be found overleaf.

3300   Gordon's 11d Return. Black print (Red G) on airforce blue.
9366   Lennox, various colours, insert Setright tickets.
0619   Weir's, black print, details written in, salmon-pink ticket.
0136   Weir's, black print, (red D) on lovat-green ticket.
1860   McMillan, black print (red 10d) on white ticket.
02356   Bannatyne Motors, black print on airforce blue.
0550   Ribbeck/CSP, stiff card railway-type red D overprint.

All the above were of a type issued 1954–on. They were 2½" x 1¼" approximately. McMillan also used lovat-green for some denominations. Lennox and Gordon used different colours for each denomination and type.

All others (except Postbus) are ATT tickets in use at various times *after* the machines issuing type No.0387 were found to be useless.

Postbus tickets (since 1977) are: Concession – white; 3p – airforce blue; 5p – light green; 10p – yellow; 20p – rust; 25p – salmon-pink; 50p – mauve. All with black print.

January, 1982. Lamlash to Brodick road almost impassable owing to snow. Alastair MacBride comes out from Brodick in a saloon car to uplift passengers for the morning steamer (three of us). Owing to the snow, the car does not get to the pier until ten minutes after departure time. Steamer still there, "singled up" ready to go, curious faces peering from the portholes at the three of us, wondering, no doubt, why the steamer should be waiting, and why the car was coming right to the gangway. We walk up the gangway and a voice from behind — Alastair — says "Another morning get out of your beds a bit earlier."

APPENDIX 2   TIMETABLES

George Shillibeer's original 1829 timetable was a very simple affair, consisting as it did of a few paragraphs in a newspaper. Since then various omnibus companies have produced a new art form in the shape of timetables. In the early days each company vied with the next to promote an image which would give them an edge by attracting the potential passengers along a shared route. During the stable period between 1930 and 1980 there have been some fantastic efforts in the field of timetable cover design. For example, there was the company who had a timetable leaflet showing Carlisle at the top with Keswick to the right of the picture-map and Durham to the left (just think about it for a moment). In 1963 another company in the south of England produced a timetable showing a highly-polished scarlet double-decker parked on a map of the south-west, a load of laughing passengers and a very jolly-looking crew are leaning against a palm tree with their boots in the sea, giggling fit to bust. The Devon General Company certainly brightened up Torquay — and all for 6d.

The first intimation of times of departures and arrivals of omni-buses in Arran in timetable form seems to have been pioneered by Ribbeck's of Brodick. Their first effort, a surviving copy of which was very kindly given to me by Mrs. Isobel Ribbeck, was on stiff card with the omnibus times on one side and tour intimations on the other under a photograph of one of their charabancs. Since then there has been an amazing number of different timetables published in the island and since, even after the 1930 Act, more than one company often shared a route — to say nothing of competing for tours which were also advertised in the timetable — there were some pretty spectacular timetables in Arran. More than one had a line drawing of a vehicle which not only did not look like anything which the company operated but did not look like anything built to conform with the Motor Vehicles (Construction & Use) Regulations. They were really weird and wonderful. All gave times of arrivals and departures of their omnibuses and some gave details of fares and times along the route. Many also served as tourist guides for the parts of the island they served and managed to convey the impression that unbearable disappointment would fall to the lot of those people tardy enough to leave booking a tour seat until the last moment.

After the mid–1960s the need to use eye-catching timetables for omnibus services no longer existed and most of them in Arran became quite restrained. For me the most impressive was the Bannatyne Motors timetable/map/guide folder which had mainly black printing on white gloss paper with black and white photographs. It folded to show a green front with black and white legend and artwork. Some of the Arran timetables are shown and described in the next few pages.

Arran Coaches timetables have always been simple affairs, by which I mean that the footnotes, exceptions and other notes are kept to a minimum although, as we shall see, this is not always a good thing. Since 1973 the company have used either a quarto or A4 size sheet, printed both sides and folded either once, to form a leaflet, or twice to form a folder as was the case with the 1974 autumn timetable. The paper varies in colour from time to time and the highlights of ATT timetables since 1973 are:

1973 red print on yellow paper, included *Round Kintyre Tour via Tarbert and Campbeltown leaving Brodick 1040 returning to Brodick at 1930. Fare £1.60.* The winter 1973/74 timetable was red print on white paper folded three times to give a narrow leaflet opening to A4 and included the reference to Duncan McAllister's 'arrangement' recorded earlier. The Kintyre tour appears to have been deleted after 1973.

1974, red on white A4 size folded three times gave the Round Arran 10A tour at 80p, with Central Arran and Evening Tour at 60p each, in addition to omnibus times.

1975 saw the withdrawal of the experimental north and south Arran departures for the early steamer. This was intimated on white quarto folded once, with brown print. Passengers from south of Whiting Bay and from north Arran requiring transport to the early steamer at 0820 were required by this table to telephone the company's office by 1700 on the Thursday in order that they might be uplifted on the Friday, the only day this facility was available. It was, in any case, discontinued later in 1975 and precise timing points, e.g. Whiting Bay *GLENASH-DALE*; Lamlash *HAMILTON TERRACE* (or *CENTRE* in pre-1974 timetables) were dropped after the summer of 1975; all subsequent timetables refer only to *WHITING BAY* and *LAMLASH*. This led to a complaint in 1977 since intending passengers assumed that the Lamlash time applied to the Monamore Bridge end of the village. As I understand it, the company — who sent a car to pick up one of the aggrieved passengers — passed the complaint on to the driver of the omnibus, Neil Black. In fact, he was not to blame, having passed the spot in question four minutes before the stated time in order to be at the centre of the village at the said stated time.

To return to the 1975 timetable, the 10A Tour was now £1.10 with the North and South Arran circular tickets at 80p each, or a combined ticket for £1.30.

The 1976 winter timetable — blue print on white quarto — advertised a new service in addition to the internal omnibus services. It was — subject to pre-booked demand for a Glasgow Excursion on Fridays in November, December, January, February and March (the last three months listed being in 1977). This excursion has been run by the company every winter since then.

The summer 1977 timetable — grey on white quarto — included Postbus times on the back page and showed the 10A Tour at £1.35. The spring and autumn timetable for that year was printed black on one side only of a foolscap sheet.

After 1978 the Postbus times were deleted from ATT tables and by 1979 the summer table — grey-green on white — A4 showed the 10A Tour at £1.75 with the North and the South Arran Circular tickets at £1.20 each, or £1.90 combined. This went up to £1.40 for the Circulars and £1.85 for the 10A in 1980 and by 1982 the black print on rust-red A4 timetables had them listed as Circulars £1.80; 10A (and, presumably, combined) £2.25. The summer 1982 timetable is remarkable in that for the first time in nearly a decade the ATT timetables were not printed on the island, but by Strathclyde Regional Council.

Brodick Pier to Brodick Castle services were listed in the 1973 and 1974 timetables showing two direct runs and utilising Lochranza-bound service omnibuses to and from the gate only, bringing it up to a total of five runs. Castle runs were not listed in 1975/76/77/78 timetables and in the case of 1977 and 1978 the Postbus table took up the space that might otherwise have been used. In 1979 there was an average of five runs each way per day to the Castle, with 'passing the gate' runs listed, and two extra runs on Wednesdays. The Castle runs only operate in summer although a Postbus leaving Brodick at 0910 makes its outward journey every day of the year via the Castle front door. The 1980 timetable of the ATT is worth going back to by virtue of the fact that it is the only one in which the company have indicated that omnibuses may be delayed and that times are subject to the arrival of the steamer. They also indicated in that year only that the 1600 from Lamlash to the south leaves from the school *and* included 1545 'light' runnings from Brodick to Lamlash.

Since they discontinued the practice of operating two omnibuses in convoy from Brodick to Whiting Bay, and following the employment of drivers in the north and west, the company have come up with a very good service making full use of existing omnibuses without 'dead' mileage being run.

Brodick Pier, Summer 1936. Omnibus about to depart from a busy scene.
Lady in bus queue: "But you must find room for me, I am a native!"
Omnibus conductress: "I don't care if you're a Zulu, there is no more room."

TIMETABLE

FOR

BRODICK - LAMLASH - WHITING BAY

AND

BRODICK - CORRIE - LOCHRANZA

AND

BRODICK - BRODICK CASTLE

BUS SERVICES

also COACH TOURS

SELF DRIVE HIRE SERVICE

PRIVATE PARTY ARRANGEMENTS

SUMMER 1967
27th MAY to 30th SEPTEMBER inclusive

ARRAN COACHES LTD.
Whiting Bay, Isle of Arran

Telephones:
Whiting Bay 240-340   Lamlash 209
Brodick 9-227

Arran
Coaches

Timetable for
ALL ARRAN
Bus Services

WINTER 1973-4
1st October 1973 until
28th April 1974

(or until further notice)

ARRAN COACHES, BRODICK
Telephone B...

1978

ISLE OF ARRAN
POSTBUS SERVICE

POST OFFICE

BRODICK - SHANNOCHIE

DEPARTURE TIMES

Mon - Sat

BRODICK	0910
BRODICK PIER	0912
CORRIEGILLS ROAD END	0913
LAMLASH	0920
KINGS CROSS ROAD END	0925
WHITING BAY	0930
DIPPEN	0943
KILDONAN SHORE PO	1220
LEVENCOROACH	1315
SHANNOCHIE PO	1220
AUCHAREOCH	*1150 & Request only
SHANNOCHIE PO	1245
LEVENCOROACH	1250
KILDONAN SHORE PO	1255
DIPPEN	1307
WHITING BAY	1310
KINGS CROSS ROAD END	1315
LAMLASH	1325
CORRIEGILLS ROAD END	1335
BRODICK PIER	1335
BRODICK	1340

On the inward journey, passengers may not be conveyed
on journeys which lie wholly within that section of
the route between Whiting Bay and Brodick

BRODICK - PIRNMILL

DEPARTURE TIMES

Mon - Sat

BRODICK	0910
860/861 JUNCTION	0913
BRODICK CASTLE	0918
CORRIE PO	0948
NORTH SANNOX	1130
LOCHRANZA	115_
PIRNMILL	1215
PIRNMILL departs	1300
LOCHRANZA	1220
NORTH SANNOX	1330
CORRIE PO	1335
BRODICK CASTLE	1345
860/861 JUNCTION	1355
BRODICK	1400

SAMPLE OF FARES

BRODICK-PIRNMILL 60p   BRODICK-SHANNOCHIE 55p
BRODICK CASTLE PIRNMILL 55p   BRODICK-AUCHAREOCH 60p
LOCHRANZA PIRNMILL 25p   WHITING BAY AUCHAREOCH 30p
For intermediate fares apply to driver

Children under 5 years travel free
Children over 5 years and under 14 years travel at
half adult fare. Fractions of a pence to be rounded up

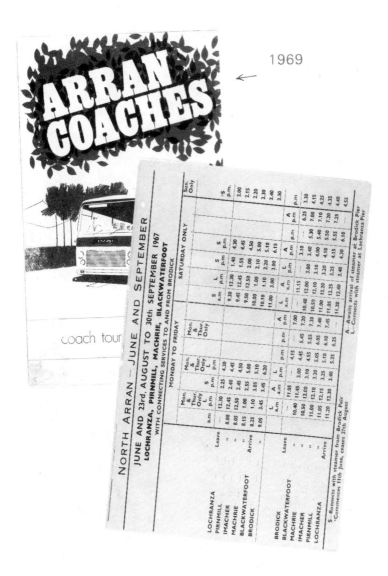

1969

NORTH ARRAN — JUNE AND SEPTEMBER

JUNE AND 23rd, AUGUST TO 30th SEPTEMBER 1967

LOCHRANZA, PIRNMILL, MACHRIE, BLACKWATERFOOT

WITH CONNECTING SERVICES TO AND FROM BRODICK

		MONDAY TO FRIDAY				SATURDAY ONLY						Sun. Only
		L a.m	Mon. & Thur. Only L a.m	S p.m	Mon. & Thur. Only L p.m	A p.m	S a.m	L a.m	S a.m	S p.m	A p.m	*S p.m
LOCHRANZA	Leave		12.30	2.25	4.30		9.30	12.30	1.40	4.30		2.00
PIRNMILL	,,		12.45	2.40	4.45		9.45	12.45	1.55	4.45		2.15
IMACHRIE	,,	8.00	12.50	2.45	4.50		9.50	12.50	2.10	4.50		2.20
MACHRIE	,,	8.05	1.00	2.55	5.00		10.00	1.00	2.10	5.00		2.30
BLACKWATERFOOT	Arrive	8.15	1.10	3.05	5.10		10.10	1.10	2.20	5.10		2.40
BRODICK	,,	8.25	3.45		6.20		11.00	3.00	3.00	6.15		3.30
		9.05										

		L a.m	A a.m	Mon. & Thur. Only S p.m	L p.m	A p.m	Mon. & Thur. Only A p.m	A p.m	L a.m	L a.m	A p.m	A p.m	A p.m
BRODICK	Leave	10.40	11.05		4.15		7.00		11.15		3.10		6.25	3.30
BLACKWATERFOOT	,,	10.50	11.45	3.00	4.45	5.45	7.20	12.00	12.00	3.00	3.40	5.30	7.00	4.15
IMACHRIE	,,	11.00	12.00	3.10	4.55	5.55	7.30	10.55	12.10	3.10	4.00	5.40	7.10	4.25
MACHRIE	,,	11.00	12.10	3.20	5.05	6.05	7.40	11.00	12.20	3.20	4.10	5.50	7.20	4.35
PIRNMILL	,,	11.05	12.15	3.25	5.10	6.10	7.45	11.05	12.25	3.25	4.15	5.55	7.25	4.40
LOCHRANZA	Arrive	11.20	12.30	3.40	5.25	6.25		11.20	12.40	3.40	4.30	6.10		4.55

S—Connects with steamer from Brodick Pier
*Commences 11th June, ceases 27th August

A—Awaits arrival of steamer at Brodick Pier
L—Connects with steamer at Lochranza Pier

coach tour

Transclyde Concessions available in 1982

APPENDIX 3   CONCESSIONARY TRAVEL

Most of the return and weekly tickets which saved money have now gone, like the individual services which issued them, and the individual passengers who used them — highly individual in the case of Greetin' Kate.

In the early 1970s the local Senior Citizen's Concession Scheme took the form of tokens, a number of which were issued to each senior citizen, each being worth three pence. As I understand it, the system allowed for as many tokens as possible to be used for a fare, that is to say, a 24 pence fare could be paid either by one token and 21 pence or by eight tokens, or by any combination in between. The tokens were metal discs, with a hole in the middle, carrying the relief legend *NATIONAL TRANSPORT TOKEN* on one side, and *TOKEN 3* on the other. They were fractionally larger than a five pence coin and when the number issued to each person had been used up there were no more issued for the rest of the year.

The tokens were replaced in 1976 by the *TRAVEL CARD*, a standard form of concession available to the elderly, the blind and the physically handicapped. No thought seems to have been given to the mentally handicapped before 1979. The cards are issued at Post Offices and are available for use on all omnibus journeys in the Strathclyde Region at off-peak times. They are issued only to Strathclyde residents and no concession card issued by other authorities and presented by holiday-makers is accepted on local services. The card allows the holder to travel the first ten miles, or any distance up to ten miles, at a reduced rate. In 1979 it was three pence, rising annually to eightpence in 1982. I am very grateful to Eloise MacDonald for her trouble in updating my 1979 copy of the explanatory leaflet. Although not flawless, it seems to me that the Strathclyde Region have devised the best of all the concessionary travel systems in Great Britain. It is well-thought-out, well-organised, well-administered and well-advertised. Short of a uniform system available in, and embracing all of Great Britain — and one can hardly blame the Strathclyde Region for the lack of it — the SRC Travel Card and its additional ferry card available to island residents on the same basis is the best to be found in this country.

The *TRAVELCARD* scheme is advertised in all post offices in the region by poster, by leaflets in a dispenser or in a pile on the counter. These leaflets, one of which is shown on page 190, were printed blue on white and folded twice to five a six-page sheet.

In the summer of 1982 a Transclyde promotion on behalf of the Strathclyde Regional Council came up with the SUMMERDAY AREA TRANSCARD, details of which are reproduced opposite, from their leaflets. This is part of what 'Transclyde' should be all about, and it is to be hoped that the scheme meets with the success it deserves. It is obviously in the experimental stage at present and no doubt it will be modified in future years. At the time of writing it is advertised in Arran only on the glass screen behind the driver's back on omnibuses 257, 258, 350 and 351 and in the pierhead offices of the Arran Transport and Trading Company — the only place from which tickets of this type can be obtained on the island. It may be that in future years, when the Regional Council overcome the problem of through-ticketing and standard ticketing and apply them to the many transport undertakings in the region, they will be obtainable from drivers in the same way that the Green Line *GOLDEN ROVER* is available from drivers. Meantime, the scheme is so much in its infancy — in Arran, at any rate — that an ATT official considered the fact that "we actually sold one this week" to be worthy of remark. Although not available on any tour operated by Arran Coaches, which is fair enough, the *SUMMERDAY* tickets are the cheapest way of seeing the island by service omnibus and no doubt the scheme, with any modifications which are found to be necessary, will become a standard option to omnibus passengers in Arran in summers to come.

Leaflets are available in company offices and take the form of a single sheet, orange, black and white gloss with an A4 size sheet in the same colours and finish folded twice to give a six-page leaflet, also available. They are also available in photocopy form. Between them they give the full details of the six different area tickets (Arran is in Area E) and the 'overall' ticket.

Any note on concessionary tickets would not be complete without a

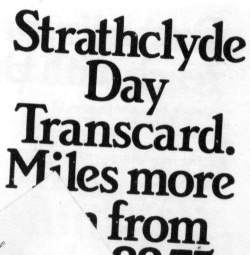

Strathclyde Day Transcard. Miles more from £2.75.

AREA E

Available on normal services operated within the area by A.A. Motor Services (Ayr), Arran Transport (Brodick), British Rail, J&J Leith (Sanquhar), J. McNair (Girvan) and Western Scottish.

Trans-Clyde

THIS IS A TRANS-CLYDE PROMOTION ON BEHALF OF STRATHCLYDE REGIONAL COUNCIL.

reference to the kindness of the ATT management in allowing half-price travel to and from work to the people employed in other parts of the island by the Youth Opportunities Programme; and to the anomaly in company regulations which allows for an omnibus to be sent out to an 'as required from . . . . ' run to pick up two scholars who have a holiday job in another part of the island, for which journey the company are unable to charge any more than the half fare applicable to scholars under 16 years of age.

A female punk rocker with orange and green hair down one side of her head boarded a bus. She asked how much the fare was to Whiting Bay. The driver replied "That will be 30p for you and 10p for the parrot."

ACKNOWLEDGEMENTS

To compile a work of this type it is necessary to call upon a great many people and ask them to recall events which happened as many as 70 years ago, some of which may not have seemed significant at the time. When I began this task I went to see Jack Lennox of The Arran Transport & Trading Company. He gave me some information and sent me to see other people who, in turn, gave me information and sent me on to others. It was rather like digging up a pyramid, the deeper I dug, the further out I had to extend. The 'dig' took me into the homes and workplaces of many Arran folk who had long since put aside all thought of the omnibuses they or their families once ran. It took me to Kirkcaldy, to Torquay, to Southampton and to Chigwell, as well as many other places and it caused a great many people to answer a lot of questions, many of which may have seemed trivial, and to search attics and chests of old photographs. For the result — this book — I am grateful to:

Mr. & Mrs. Donnie Lennox, John Henderson, Isobel, Ernest, Sandy, Bessie and Henry Ribbeck, Campbell Armit, Archie Currie, Mary Hodge, Mrs. W. Bannatyne, Joe Hartley, Norman Sillars, 'Boyda' Milton, Mrs. E. McLeod, Billy Gilmour, Sheila Kerr, Mrs. D. Auchinvole, Alistair Hamilton, Annie Aitken, Mr. & Mrs. C. Cook, Gavin Cook, Bess MacMillan, Jimmy Kelso, Maimie Smith, Mrs. W. Urie, Alexander Buick, Tom Alexander, Mrs. J. Davidson, Rab Hume, Len Smith, Archie 'Ro' Robertson and Don White. Robert Haddow, David Warwick, Jack Lennox, Bob Miller, George Bannatyne, Margaret Aitken, Grant Weir, Danny Stewart, Donny Campbell, John Smith, Neil Black, George Munro, Colin Cox, Fergy Latona, Alastair MacBride, John Busby, Ralston Green, Clive Ridley, Bruce Hough, Phil Currie, Phil Broomhead, Andy Lane, Kevin Kilshaw, Margaret Murchie, Alistair Nicholson, Chrystina Cruszecka, Elizabeth Arnott, Frank Hamilton, Charlie Hendry, Budgie Bremner and Alistair MacKenzie. Ian Miller, Joe Edgar, Sandy Gauld, Bill Dickie, Roy Dickie, Louis Joss, Stewart Black, Danny Craig, George McKechnie (both of them), Andy Knox, Jimmy Murchie, Neil Southgate, Neil Kerr, Sal Bannatyne, Jean Lane, Ruth Young, Alice Lennox, Cathy MacKenzie, Donald McQueen and Mr. D. F. Francey of the Post Office. Paul Monty, Mo Khan, Marc Head, Ronnie Mann and John Millar, Fred Robson and Tom Finnie. Kate and Ernest Gordon, Alexander 'Ching' Hamilton, Wynn Barbour, Ian Young, Matt Kerr, Grace, Mary, Rena and Jimmy Cannon, Stella MacRae, Mrs. M. Kelso, May Greenhalgh, Ross MacKenzie, Johnny Miller, Sandy Duncan, Douglas Kerr, Tom Scott, Walter Marshall, David Oakes, James Fyffe (Monte Rey), Tom Graham, Geoff Norris, Ian Young and Jimmy Jeffries. Mr. & Mrs. R. B. Haddow, Snr., Alan Cook and John MacKenzie, Tom Paterson, David Hamilton, Dennis Turner, Ella Lennox, Dave McLellan, Kek Arnott, Mrs. I. Mackenzie, Robert MacKenzie, Ian and Janette MacKenzie, Steve Gill, George Mathieson, Jenny Stewart, Allan Currie, Peter and Rosemary Jowsey and Harry Bowden. Allan and Donald McNeill, Charles Ash, Paul Gledhill, Finlay Snr., Robin, Willie and Finlay Jnr. Cook, Ian Walters, Ken & Chrissie Wolverton and George Lyle. Mr. & Mrs. J. McKinnon, Janet Mulholland, Andrew Hamilton, Donald Stewart, John Adamson, John and Laura Murchie, (thanks again for the soup, Laura). Lawrence and Robin Crawford, D.S. Bannatyne, D.E. Bannatyne, J. S. Bannatyne, Willie James, Jimmy and Mrs. Jimmy Bannatyne, Mrs. J. Currie, Colin A. and Isabel Currie (thanks for the coffee and cream cakes), Willie Anderson and Willie Robertson. D.G.Weir, Donald MacNiven and Margaret Hood. Dougie Munro, Johnny Anderson, Peter McMillan, Neil Dawtry, Ricky MacDonald, Alistair Gordon, Finlay Kerr-Newton and Neil Clark. Miss I.Young, Jack Logan. Hamilton Kerr, Ian Martin, Ian MacNaught, Bill and Babs McQuattie, M.Morton Hunter, Robert Clow, T.McLure, the Mitchell Library staff in Glasgow, Dave & Gael Hearn, Gavin Booth, Sue Reeves, Liz Williams, Mrs.K.McColl and Mrs. D. Middleton, Lily Powell and Cathy Craske. Duncan Weir, Rothesay Motor Licence Office, Ian Allen Ltd., London Transport, Devon General (Western National) Douglas Haigh, Cumberland Motor Services and their historian, David Griserthwaite, Joan Hampshire and the Rev.R.B.Nikon-Cooper, the PROs of Ford, Vauxhall Motors, Hestair-Dennis, Chrysler, Arthur Guthrie & Sons Ltd., Jennie Drinkell and Margaret Harris.

Between them they have provided information and photographs and I am very grateful to them all. Some, like Ernest Ribbeck, Donny Lennox and Donald Stewart went to a lot of trouble to ensure that I had all the photographs I needed and all the facts I wanted (and to ensure that I'd got those facts right!). Some, like Bob Grieves, travelled (I estimate) 95 miles to do so. Some, like Joan Hampshire who looked up the correct title of the Shillibeer development when I telephoned her — first time she'd heard from me in ten years, what a nerve I've got — to fill in a blank space. My thanks, too, to George T. Waugh, Robert Gilligan and Rosemary Walker. I am grateful to them all.

PHOTOGRAPHS

It is conventional — one might say that it is elementary courtesy — to 'credit' the person who supplies a copy of a photograph for use in a book, even if it is a copy of a photograph taken by, or for, someone else, and the copyright period has expired. This is usually done by incorporating the name of the supplier into the caption.

Many of the people who have gone to great trouble to provide me with photographs may wonder why I have not had the courtesy to credit them in the accepted way. No discourtesy is intended. The fact is that in many cases the same photograph was offered to me by several people. Then, when it comes to inserting the photograph, does one give the credit for it to the first person who offered it, or to the last person? So, I have compromised, and all of those who were kind enough to supply photographs, duplicates or not, it does not matter to me, are listed along with the people who supplied the information.

The dates I have given in the captions to some of the photographs may be misleading. Stewart's Motors 1937 Bedford, for instance, refers to the date on which the vehicle was built, not the date on which the photograph was taken. The precise date was not ascertainable. With other photographs it was possible to be more precise. The photograph of Hamilton's horse-brake at the Lagg Hotel is a case in point, this photograph having been specially commissioned to commemorate the first day of operation in 1889.

The up-to-date photographs are not intended to be just of the vehicles they depict. There are only two photographs of ATT351 and of Postbus 717, for instance. The many other photographs in which 351, 717 or, indeed, any other vehicles appear are photographs of the scenery through which the services pass, the roads on and conditions under which they operate. While they do feature vehicles which are depicted elsewhere, the photographs are intended, in these cases, to be an overall picture, *including*, not *of* a coach or omnibus.

First round the houses.

First round the clock.

In 1946, the Royal Bank was first in Britain to introduce mobile banking. (We still operate 16 Mobile Branches today.)

Thirty years on, in 1977, we became the first Scottish bank to introduce 24 hour on-line cash dispensers. Cashline is now a household name.

It's service like this, throughout our long history, that has made us first with our customers.

From the smallest account holder to the biggest business.

Because most people prefer a bank that's leading to one that's merely following.

The Royal Bank

The Royal Bank of Scotland plc incorporates The Royal Bank of Scotland, The Commercial Bank of Scotland Limited and The National Bank of Scotland Limited.

SCOTIA SCOTTISH TOURS
56 Bothwell Street, Glasgow
Telephone: 041 248 3177

This is your holiday programme

SATURDAY Glasgow to Brodick
Touring Coach departs from 56 Bothwell Street, Glasgow at 13.30, travelling direct to Ardrossan. Your Coach will travel with you on the car ferry from Ardrossan to Brodick and deliver you and your luggage to your Hotel thus eliminating any difficulty in the handling of luggage, so often associated with island holidays. You will arrive at your Hotel before 17.00 in good time for dinner.

SUNDAY Central Arran
Your Coach will call for you after lunch for your first tour of the Island. The roads on Arran have good surfaces and are suitable for Coach travel of a pleasant leisurely nature, the many bends and gradients offering ever changing beauty. This circular tour is westward by the String Road returning to the east coast by the Ross Road to Lamlash.

MONDAY Campbeltown
Whole Day Tour to Campbeltown. By coach from Brodick to Lochranza where the Kilbrannan Sound will be crossed by car ferry to Claonaig, for a circular tour of the Mull of Kintyre viewing the Atlantic Islands of Islay and Gigha and the mountains of Jura. A stop will be made for Lunch at Campbeltown. The return to Brodick offers magnificent views of the Island of Arran across the Kilbrannan Sound.

TUESDAY Arran Circular
Whole day circular tour of the Island of Arran by the Coast road through the villages of Corrie, Sannox, Pirnmill and Machrie to Blackwaterfoot. After lunch the return journey is by Slidery with its modern Cheese Creamery, Kildonan and Whiting Bay.

WEDNESDAY Free day
Day of leisure. For the more active, sporting facilities at Brodick include, golf, bowling, tennis, putting, rowing, sea angling and burn fishing. The beach offers over a mile of uncrowded golden sand.

THURSDAY South Arran
Your Coach will again call for you after lunch for a circular tour of the south end of the island allowing time for shopping at Lamlash and Whiting Bay returning by the villages of Lagg and Shiskine.

FRIDAY Brodick Castle
Afternoon visit by Coach to Brodick Castle with its famous gardens. This former home of the Duchess of Montrose which dates from the fourteenth century is now under the care of the National Trust for Scotland, and has many priceless exhibits of great interest.

SATURDAY Glasgow via Gourock
Your Coach will leave your Hotel after breakfast for the sail to Ardrossan and returning to Glasgow by the picturesque coast of the Firth of Clyde by West Kilbride, Largs, Wemyss Bay, to Gourock and by the River Clyde to arrive Glasgow by 12.30.

BOOKS FROM KILBRANNAN

THE BOOK OF ARRAN
Volume I: Archaeology
Volume II: History & Folklore
A reprint of the two famous reference books first published at the beginning of the century by The Arran Society of Glasgow.
Set of two volumes (Hardback) £40.00   *ISBN 0 907939 04 X*

CASTLES IN THE AIR by Lady Jean Fforde
The story of a childhood in Brodick Castle and Buchanan Castle describing the visits of Prince Rainier and Princess Antoinette of Monaco and a way of life which is gone forever. Dozens of photographs.
Hardback £8.50   *ISBN 0 907939 01 5*

ARRAN: AN ISLAND'S STORY by Allan Paterson Milne
A popular history of post-Clearance Arran. Anecdotes and historical fact, with a detailed account of the Goatfell murder.
Paperback £2.50   *ISBN 0 907939 00 7*

EXPLORING ARRAN'S PAST by Dr. Horace Fairhurst
An enlarged and revised edition of the popular archaeological guide to Arran.
Paperback £3.00   *ISBN 0 907939 05 8*

AVAILABLE FROM BOOKSELLERS
OR DIRECT FROM THE PUBLISHERS

Kilbrannan Publishing Limited
Ivy Cottage
Brodick, Isle of Arran
Telephone: Brodick (0770) 2539